D1537022

Eskimo Dolls

Edited by Suzi Jones

Essay, ''Eskimo Dolls,'' by Susan W. Fair

Dollmaker photographs by Rob Stapleton

Doll photographs by Chris Arend

Published by the Alaska State Council on the Arts

Published on the occasion of a traveling exhibition sponsored by the Alaska State Council on the Arts

© 1982 by the Alaska State Council on the Arts. All rights reserved.

Fourth printing. June 1993.

Alaska State Council on the Arts
411 West 4th Avenue, Suite 1E, Anchorage, Alaska 99501-2343

Library of Congress Catalog Number: 82-620026

ISBN 0-910615-00-4

Contents

Introduction by Suzi Jones...4

The Dollmakers and the Dolls...7

''Eskimo Dolls'' by Susan W. Fair...45

Bibliography...72

Introduction

Over the past few years in Alaska, conferences with Native artists, a survey on Native arts programming, and meetings around the state with people interested in Native arts have repeatedly emphasized the need for more exhibits of Alaska Native art. In particular, people want to see exhibits capable of traveling to rural villages in Alaska. *Eskimo Dolls* is a direct response to that expressed need. *Eskimo Dolls* features the work of eighteen Inupiat, Yup'ik, Cup'ik, and St. Lawrence Island Yup'ik dollmakers in a traveling exhibit, and in this catalog published for the exhibit.

The Eskimo doll project began with recommendations from the Traditional Native Arts Panel to the State Arts Council in the summer of 1981 to produce a Native art exhibit which could travel to Alaskan villages. In the fall of 1981, Susan W. Fair carried out research for the arts council to identify Eskimo dollmakers actively pursuing their art. Then, through a cooperative agreement with the Alaska Native Foundation's Alaska Native Crafts Program, twenty dollmakers were commissioned to create work for the exhibit. (Two of those originally commissioned, Pansy Omwari, Nome, and Elizabeth Lampe, Barrow, were unble to make dolls within our project dates because of unexpected illness in one case and other commitments in the other, and we regret not being able to show their fine work in the exhibit.) The selection of the dollmakers was difficult. There are many more talented dollmakers in Alaska than the eighteen featured here. Over all, the exhibit has tried to show not only some of the finest work being done today by Eskimo dollmakers, but also attempts to represent several regional styles of dollmaking which were identified in the research, such as those styles from Eek, Kotzebue and Shishmaref. The dolls also represent the incredible variety of materials used by the Alaska Native artists and the traditional methods of preparation of these materials.

The methods used in selecting dollmakers included the persual of museum collections, particularly those of the Alaska State Museum, Anchorage Historical and Fine Arts Museum, and the University of Alaska Museum at Fairbanks. Equally important was the examination of dolls in the homes of many Anchorage collectors. These people kindly racked their journals and memories for information about dolls sometimes collected years ago. Dollmakers themselves often suggest other artists they knew, and so, word of mouth and friend-of-friends, became an important and appropriate part of the selection process. Bush radio hotlines and personal letters were also sent to dollmakers, a dozen of whom sent examples of their work to State Arts Council offices.

Sadly, it is likely that many talented dollmakers in rural Alaska remain virtually unknown and are not represented here. In addition, many trendsetters and tradition bearers in the dollmaking field were found to be in such poor health that they could no longer sew, or are no longer living. Hazel Omwari of Gambell, who made the Siberian baby doll style, and award-winning dollmaker Anna Kungurkak of Toksook Bay, are no longer able to make dolls. Louise Tall of Hooper Bay makes only a few, as do Lena Sours of Kotzebue and Emma Black of Anchorage. Ethel Washington, pioneer dollmaker of the Kotzebue tradition, and Irene Hawley, also of Kotzebue, are no longer living. Jeanette Noongwook, who was an early maker of the realistic ivory doll type from Savoonga, died 1981; and Alice Moore, who made exceptional painted wood-faced dolls, died in Twin Hills several years ago.

In the spring of 1982, while the dollmakers were working on dolls for the exhibit, we traveled to each of their homes to talk with them about dolls and dollmaking and to photograph them at work in their own environments. Susan Fair interviewed dollmakers in northwest Alaska, Suzi Jones in southwest Alaska, and Rob Stapleton photographed each dollmaker. The finished dolls were all photographed for us by Chris Arend in his Anchorage studio. As Susan Fair notes of her fieldwork experiences: "Dollmakers took us in, fed us, drove us a mile or more to village airstrips, and put up with endless questions that were hopefully not too impolite, but may have been boring to those so well acquainted with the process of dollmaking . . . . Some dimensions of the project cannot be captured with pen or camera, like the twinkle in Margaret Ahlalook's eye as she pulled stuffing for her dolls out of the cushions of her couch, or the earthy smell and oily feel of Mary Nash's Arctic loonskin doll. At ten p.m. on CB radio channel five in Anaktuvuk Pass, we were treated to traditional stories about caribou hunting in Inupiaq, kindly translated by George Paneak. Channel five is the storytelling channel for the village, and it is in use every night. Some dollmakers, notably Caroline Penayah, Dolly Spencer, and Annie Alowa, gave us one-woman marathons on dollmaking and seemed to enjoy telling it as much as we enjoyed listening . . . . The doll project, for those of us who worked on it, has been a living, breathing process—not always easy, but clearly worthwhile. Emma Olanna of Shishmaref expressed some concern over the longevity of the project: 'What if we pass away before we reach that catalog?' Sometimes, all of us felt the same way, but I hope that Emma, and all the other Native people without whom this project could not have existed, are pleased with the final product.''

The tapes, transcripts and translations of interviews, along with all the negatives and slides from the fieldwork will be deposited for permanent storage in the Arctic and Polar Regions Collection of the Rasmuson Library at the University of Alaska at Fairbanks. It is our hope that these materials will form the nucleus of a collection of documentary materials on Alaska's Native artists—a subject on which there is far too little information. We discovered in the course of our research, for instance, that there was practically no information on Eskimo dolls, other than a few brief references in more general works on Eskimo art. Thus, we hope this catalog, with its fine essay by Susan W. Fair, will fill a significant void in Native art scholarship, and that the materials in the Rasmuson Library will be of benefit to those in the future who wish to know about Native arts and culture in Alaska.

There have been a great many people who have worked very hard in the course of this project, and I should like to acknowledge their contributions. Of course, our greatest appreciation goes to the dollmakers themselves, not only for making such wonderful dolls for us, but also for allowing us to intrude in their lives for a while and for sharing their knowledge of dollmaking so freely with us.

There are also other men and women who assisted with our fieldwork, either as interpreters or in providing interviews and information themselves, and we would like to thank Clement Ungott, Irma Ungott and Eva Tungiyan of Gambell; George Paneak and Elija Kakinya in Anaktuvuk Pass; Flora Imergan, George Noongwook, Christine Alowa, Nelson Alowa, Theresa

Rookoook Kava and Judy Pelowook in Savoonga; Herbert Anungazuk and Helen Okpealuk in Wales; Esau Weyiouanna, Johnson Eningowuk, Lucy Eningowuk, Amos Kiyutelluk, Anna Pootoogooluk and Jack Herman Ningealook in Shishmaref; Martina Panik in Wainwright; Joe Friday, Joe Slats, Tony Umugak and Mary Pingayak in Chevak; Godlieva Barr and Liz Ali in Bethel; Natalia Smith, Neva Rivers, Frank Keim and Bruce Tillitt in Hooper Bay; Mary Azean in Kongiganak; Alice Foster, Marie White, Martha Carter and Susie Brown's daughter, Annie, in Eek; and Sarah Tweet in Anchorage. Thanks also go to April Varnell in Bethel, Gil and Sophie Gutierrez in Chevak and Frank Keim in Hooper Bay, who generously provided fieldworkers in southwest Alaska with bed and board during their travels.

Curators, collectors and art dealers who assisted us in our research include Larry Bracken and Bette Hulbert of the Alaska State Museum; Walter Van Horn and Cay Cloe at the Anchorage Historical and Fine Arts Museum; Dinah Larsen at the University Museum in Fairbanks; Peter Corey of the Sheldon Jackson Museum, Sitka; Alaska Native Arts and Crafts in Anchorage; Dixie Rynearson of Sitka; Ralph Ring of Frontier Tanning; Kathy Schwartz; Donna Hobson; Mary Fran Barkshire; Marianne Fitzgerald; Jan Fallico; Karen Vogeler of the Alaska Native Hospital Gift Shop; Eleanor Klingel; Lint and Kay Moustakis; Norma; Hoyt; Ross and Becky Clement; Eileen Uy Jekil and Jo Michalski.

Special thanks are also due Irene Reed of the Alaska Native Language Center at the University of Alaska, Fairbanks; Larry Hood and Jim Hogue of the U.S. Department of the Interior, Fish and Wildlife; Bill Schneider of the Oral History Program, Rasmuson Library, University of Alaska, Fairbanks; the Institute of Alaska Native Arts, and Charlene Johnston.

The eloquent photography of Rob Stapleton and Chris Arend speaks for itself in this catalog and, in decades to come, will constitute an important visual record of Alaska Native art. Susan Fair has invested much more of herself in this project than is ever accounted for by a contract or revealed in an essay. Her previous knowledge of Alaska Native art was invaluable, and her commitment to the project was coupled with a very personal commitment to the dollmakers themselves—a care and concern for each individual that continually affirmed the very human side of the project.

The Alaska State Museum has willingly taken on *Eskimo Dolls* as part of their traveling exhibit program so that it can be seen in many communities throughout the state over the next few years. The exhibit was designed and fabricated by Presentation Design Group, working with the very Alaskan and practical instructions that it must all be able to fit into a Cessna 207. This catalog owes its handsome appearance to the design staff of Clark Mishler and Associates.

We deeply appreciate the efforts of all those who have contributed their talents to this project, and I apologize for any names that we have missed in our thanks. *Eskimo Dolls* has been a major endeavor for the Traditional Native Arts Program over the last two years, and it is our hope that it will provide some small measure of recognition for those women and men who, with knowledge and skill of their art and with respect for the traditions of their own ancient cultures, create Eskimo dolls.

This map locates the villages of the Eskimo dollmakers and shows three Eskimo linguistic and cultural regions in Alaska.

5

The Dollmakers
and the Dolls

Mary Black

Yup'ik, Kongiganak

Coiled Basketry Dolls, Male is
15-7/8″ x 9″; female is 13″ x 8-5/8″.

Coiled grass basketry dolls represent a
relatively recent art form and testify to
the basketmaker's creativity and skill in
responding to the market. Mary Black
prefers to make baskets, but does make
the much more difficult basketry dolls
upon request. Preparation of materials
used in these dolls is complex and time
consuming, from picking, curing and
drying of the grass to the hunting of the
seal for the seal gut, which must then be
scraped, soaked, cleaned, dried and
dyed to be used as decoration on the
coils of grass.

Materials: Coiled beach grass. Male doll
has clothing denoted by areas of grass
colored with commercial dyes; mittens
are clipped calf skin. Female doll has
mouton hair, rabbit fur ruff on parka
with yarn ties, clipped calf skin mittens;
decoration on clothing consists of strips
of dyed seal intestine and dyed grass.

Rosalie Paniyak, with her son

Cup'ik, Chevak

Going to the Mud House for a Party,
27½″ x 10½″.

Rosalie Paniyak is one of the most innovative Eskimo dollmakers. Her dolls are known for their witty, whimsical, and sometimes macabre faces which typically have long pointed noses and chins, with beads for teeth and eyes. Paniyak is one among several Chevak dollmakers whose work contributes to the development of a distinctive regional style over the past decade. These dolls are characterized by their expressive skin faces with individual, often humorous expressions, and by their poses—they are depicted performing traditional everyday actions such as trapping, gathering eggs, filling a seal poke, or "going to the mud house for a party."

Materials: Seal skin face with appliqued nose, glass marble eyes, seed bead teeth, badger hair; bearded seal intestine rain parka; spotted seal mittens and straps; spotted seal skin boots with bearded seal soles; corduroy pants; cloth body stuffed with rags. The dishes are of coiled beach grass.

Mary Nash

Cup'ik, Chevak

Wintertime Seal Hunter,
23½ " x 10¼ ".

This doll's parka is an older style, loon skin parka. Loons are only one of several birds known to be used in bird skin parkas in historic times. Other birds commonly used for clothing include murre, puffin, cormorant and guillemot. Bird skin parkas are light, waterproof, and extremely warm. Dollmaker Mary Nash says people long ago liked to sew with loon skins because the skin did not tear easily and because the feathers had nice designs. This doll, dressed in a loon skin parka, represents a man who is a skilled hunter. Today, federal laws prohibit the sale of items with feathers from migratory birds, and a special permit from U.S. Fish and Wildlife made possible the inclusion of a doll with traditional bird skin clothing in this exhibit.

Materials: Carved wood (bark) face with pencil, ink and aluminum foil features; Arctic loon skin parka and hood; spotted seal skin mittens and boots with bearded seal soles; carved wood ice tester and paddle. The doll's cloth body is stuffed with grass.

Susie Brown

Yup'ik, Eek

Doll Family, group is 12″ x 11½″.

This family of four is Susie Brown's presentation of the classic oval-faced wood doll made in Eek and a few nearby villages. This doll type was originated in the 1940's by Stella Cleveland of Eek and today is being made by at least fifteen women in the village. In this family, the mother is holding the youngest child, while the boy grasps a bat and ball and the father has a seal from a recent hunt.

Materials: All have carved wood faces with painted features; rabbit fur parkas with white calf, yarn, and seed bead trim. Mother and children have sheep skin hair; father and son have beaver hats with yarn ties. Mukluks are seal with leather soles. Other trim includes beaver, otter, and clipped calf. The cloth bodies are stuffed with paper. The boy's bat is a mink bone, and the ball is leather.

Lou C. Brown

Yup'ik, Eek

Old Man and Woman, each doll is 11½ ″ x 5¼ ″.

The first ''old people'' dolls were made in the 1970's by Grace White in Eek. This style of doll with white hair and wrinkled face, quickly gained popularity among Eek's dollmakers and today is one of two major doll types in the village. (The other type is the wood faced doll, exemplified in this exhibit by the Susie Brown dolls.)

Materials: Deer skin faces with embroidered features, sheep skin hair; rabbit fur parkas with beaver trim, raccoon ruffs, leather, yarn and seed bead trim; ringed seal skin mukluks with deer skin soles. Dolls are sewn with waxed thread, stuffed with tissue paper and cotton, with rolled cardboard in legs. Skins are commercially tanned, purchased at the village store and by mail order.

Helen H. Smith

Yup'ik, Hooper Bay

Yup'ik Dance Scene, each figure is 12″ x 7½″.

Dancing has historically been an important part of Eskimo ceremonial and recreational life. Though the influence of early missionaries destroyed the tradition of dance in many villages, in others, such as Hooper Bay, Eskimo dance is still a dynamic tradition. In this typical Yu'pik dance scene, a singer beats a skin drum while two women and a man dance. The women wear wolf headdresses and hold dance fans; the man, who dances from a kneeling position in front of the women, also uses hand fans decorated with feathers.

Materials: Commercially tanned leather faces with embroidered features; rabbit fur parkas with trim of wolf, wolverine, sheep skin, beaver, calf skin, and beads; boots are ringed seal skin or leather with leather soles. Doll bodies are wire wrapped with cloth, bound with string. Women's headdresses are bleached seal skin bands with wolf fur, sheep skin, yarn, cloth, Arctic ground squirrel, leather, and seed beads. Hands are of cloth, and dance fans are wolf fur, feathers and beads. The drum has a wood handle and seal intestine stretched over a plastic lid. Wire frames enable dolls' arms and legs to be moved to any position.

Martina Oscar

Yup'ik, Bethel (originally Nelson Island—Newtok, Tununak)

Man Attaching Corkline to Gillnet,
5″ tall; base 4″ x 5½″.

Activity dolls (or doll models, as they are also called) are regularly made by at least six dollmakers in different regions of Alaska. The Yukon-Kuskokwim State Fair in Bethel even has a separate judging category for ''activity dolls.'' This small doll, posed mid-action, may well be a direct descendant of the miniature dolls Martina and many other women of her generation in southwest Alaskan villages played with as young girls. Activity dolls are posed in traditional ac- tivities of work and play, from mending nets to fishtrap making, dancing, berry picking and many others.

Materials: Wood base, post and stump; corduroy body and pants; cloth parka with northern fur seal ruff; commercially tanned leather face with embroidered features; leather boots with cloth trim, leather soles; driftwood pipe, net floats and net needle; lead net weights; string net and lines.

Josephine Ungott

St. Lawrence Island Siberian Yup'ik, Gambell

Male Hunter, 15″ x 8-3/4″.
Female in Fancy Parka 15″ x 11″.

Bird skins and feathers have been used by Eskimos for parkas and for ornamentation at least as early as the Birnik culture period (500-1000 A.D.) and until quite recently into the early twentieth century. Nowadays, however, enforcement of federal laws prohibiting the sale or trade of migratory bird feathers have eliminated most sewing with these materials. These two dolls dressed in very traditional parkas, one of cormorant neck skins and the other decorated with auklet crests, were produced for this exhibit under a special permit from the U.S. Fish and Wildlife Service.

Materials: (Male Hunter) Winter-bleached seal skin face with embroidered, appliqued features; leather head; cloth body and cotton stuffing; cormorant neck skin parka with seal skin trim, mink ruff; ringed seal skin patns and mittens; dyed seal skin mukluks with bearded seal soles, braided sinew ties, bleached seal skin boot straps, belt, scabbard, hunting pack and rifle case.

Materials: (Female in Fancy Parka) Winter-bleached seal skin face with embroidered, appliqued features, yarn hair, seed bead trim; cloth head and body with cotton stuffing; seal skin undergarments. Parka is winter-bleached bearded seal intestine with fringe of unborn seal at cuffs and botton, seal trim on hood; parka ornamentation consists of narrow strips of alder and crepe paper-dyed walrus stomach and the maxillae and topknots of 122 crested auklets.

Floyd and Amelia Kingeekuk

St. Lawrence Island Siberian Yup'ik, Savoonga

St. Lawrence Island Man in Windproof,
12″ x 6½″.

This St. Lawrence Island man is wearing
an old style windproof or dress shirt,
made of bleached walrus intestine. His
hair style is one that was common in
many Eskimo villages several generations
ago. The finely detailed carving on the
head and hands of this doll are typical of
Floyd Kingeekuk's work. The right hand
is hinged at the wrist so that it can be
moved 360°.

Materials: Walrus ivory head and hands
with incised and painted features, rabbit
fur hair, seal hair moustache; bleached
walrus intestine parka wth alder (or cinnabar)-dyed border and rabbit fur trim;
cloth inner parka; seal skin pants; alder-
dyed seal skin boots with bleached seal
skin straps and tops, bearded seal soles;
cloth body with cotton stuffing; wood
staff.

Annie Alowa, with grandchildren

St. Lawrence Island Siberian Yup'ik, Savoonga

St. Lawrence Island Favorite Daughter,
12″ x 7¼ ″.

This doll's beaded, braided hairstyle is one that dollmaker Annie Alowa says was worn by ''favored daughters.'' This doll has a fancy reindeer fawn skin parka, and her ivory face and hands are incised with tatoos, a tradition seen now only among the oldest generation of St. Lawrence Island women. The doll's accessories include a seal intestine sewing bag with fur scraps and sinew, a wood tray for cutting meat and a tiny ulu and seal skin scraper.

Materials: Carved ''fossil'' walrus ivory head and hands, engraved and painted tattoos and features; wolverine tail hair with seed bead trim; reindeer fawn skin parka with winter-bleached seal skin trim, colored embroidery floss, yarn, wolverine fur dangles, beaver cuffs and trim, and wolf and wolverine ruff; reindeer fawn leg mukluks with leather soles, beaver trim. Scrap bag is seal intestine with miscellaneous fur scraps and sinew thread. Tray is carved wood with miniature seal skin scraper and woman's knife.

Vincent and Molly Tocktoo, with grandaughter Lynette Hannah Turner

Inupiat, Shishmaref

Reindeer Horn Dolls, each doll is
6″ x 1-3/4″.

The tradition of making reindeer horn
dolls originated in Shishmaref and gained popularity in the 1930's when the
opening of a village Native store created
a demand for the dolls for the tourist
trade. Today many men and women in
Shishmaref make horn dolls which are
sold locally and by mail order. Horn
dolls, more than any other contemporary
dolls, resemble the small carved human
figures found in northwest Alaska in the
nineteenth century.

Materials: Clothed dolls are dressed in
seal skin pants, calf skin boots with felt
and leather trim, Arctic ground squirrel
parkas with alder-dyed reindeer skin and
calf skin trim; squirrel belly mittens.

Elliot Olanna

Inupiat, Shishmaref

Whalebone Family, father, 7-7/8″ x 2-7/8″; mother, 6-3/4″ x 2-3/4″; son, 3-3/4″ x 2-3/4″.

This family of whalebone figures represents one of three types of dolls produced in the village of Shishmaref. Whalebone dolls are usually carved by men, while both men and women collaborate on reindeer horn dolls and "stuffed" (soft) dolls with ivory faces. The whalebone used for carving comes from old pieces of whalebone washed up on the beach and gathered by people in the springtime. Whalebone is used for

sculpture, both large and small, representational and abstract, by Shismaref artists.

Materials: Old whalebone, painted features, clothing defined by relief carving.

Maggie Komonaseak

Inupiat, Wales

Packing Doll, 10″ x 7¼″.

"Packing dolls," Eskimo doll mothers carrying infants against their backs inside the hoods of their parkas, are a doll type common to several northern Alaskan villages, including Wales and Shishmaref. This particular doll style, with an ivory face sewn on to a cloth head, is found mainly in Wales, although its prototype may have originated in Siberia. Although Maggie Komonaseak does not remember playing with dolls as a child, she does recall that she and her friends often played mother by packing rocks or puppies in their parkas.

Materials: Carved walrus ivory faces with engraved, inked features; seal skin parka and mukluks with rabbit fur ruff and border and trim of leather with seed beads and felt; head is Arctic ground squirrel; mittens are leather; body is cloth and reindeer hair stuffing.

Margaret Ahlalook

Inupiat, Wainwright

Hunter and Woman with Baby, hunter, 10½ ″ x 5¼ ″; mother and baby, 10½ ″ x 4-7/8″.

Caribou is one of the prime materials for cold climate clothing. It is light in weight, provides optimum warmth, and is durable. This man and woman are dressed in caribou parkas and pants, with the woman's parka designed to accomodate her young child in back. The seal skin used for faces and trim has been bleached white by a special cold weather tanning process. This winter-bleached seal skin is often used in fancy work in Northwest Alaska.

Materials: Bleached seal skin faces with appliqued noses and embroidered features; barren ground caribou parkas and pants; winter bleached seal skin boot tops, parka trim, belt and mitten straps with thread and dyed seal skin ornamentation; calf skin boots and mittens; boot straps are leather, hunter's parka ruff is unborn seal, woman's ruff is mink, scarves are felt, harpoon is walrus ivory. The dolls' bodies are calico with synthetic stuffing. (When asked about the stuffing Margaret Ahlalook burst into laughter and pointed to a nearby sofa cushion.)

Susie Paneak

Inupiat, Anaktuvuk Pass

Hunter Doll, 20″ x 10″.

This doll comes from Anaktuvuk Pass, located in the heart of the spectacular Brooks Range. Nearby herds of roving barren ground caribou form the mainstay of lifestyles and diet for this village. Paneak's doll embodies the importance of this animal to the region. The doll is crafted almost exclusively from caribou, inside and out. His face is a miniaturization of the popular molded caribou skin masks which originated in this village and are now widely sold to tourists and collectors.

Materials: Molded barren ground caribou skin face with caribou lashes, black bear beard and hair. Caribou clothing with wolf ruff and belt, calf skin and beaver trim. Wood staff; all other materials including the body stuffing are caribou.

Caroline Penayah

St. Lawrence Island Siberian Yup'ik, Copper Center (originally Savoonga)

St. Lawrence Island Woman in Qallevak, 10½″ x 6″.

Originally a Siberian design, the *qallevak*, or one-piece suit, was usually made of reindeer fawn skin or seal skin. Caroline Penayah remembers seeing older women in her family wearing these *sutis* when she was a child. The braids with loops of beads and the bleached seal skin mukluks with red, alder-dyed trim are still worn by some women for special occasions on St. Lawrence Island.

Materials: Winter-bleached seal skin face with embroidered features, synthetic hair, seed beads; pieced, dyed seal skin suit with coyote ruff and cuffs; leather ties; pony bead trim; mukluks are winter bleached seal skin with alder-dyed caribou esophagus trim and bearded seal soles; leather body; carved walrus ivory hands.

Eva Heffle

Inupiat, Fairbanks (originally Kotzebue)

Blanket Toss, base, 14" square; each doll is 8" x 3".

The blanket toss is a popular event at Eskimo celebrations such as the annual Eskimo Indian Olympics or the Savoonga Walrus Carnival. The "blanket" is usually a walrus or bearded seal hide. This blanket toss scene is only one of thirty-two scenes in Eva Heffle's repertoire of carefully detailed activity dolls.

Materials: Dolls have wood faces with seed bead eyes, painted features, sheep skin or synthetic hair and cloth bodies. Clothing includes ringed seal, muskrat, beaver, rabbit, winter-bleached seal skin, leather, corduroy, calico, synthetic fibers, rickrack trim. "Blanket" is walrus hide. Base has sand glued on plywood

Dolly Spencer

Inupiat, Homer (originally Kotzebue)

*Traditionally Dressed Eskimo Lady Doll,
Above Arctic Circle Style,* 15 ¾ " x 7 ".

Dolly Spencer dolls epitomize the art of
Eskimo dollmaking for many collectors
and museums. Dolly Spencer has won
many awards for her dolls, and she is un-
paralleled in her attention to craftsmanship and minute detail. She carries on
the dollmaking tradition begun by Lena
Sours and Ethel Washington in
Kotzebue in the late 1930's. Often her
dolls are portraits of people she admires
or has known. This doll represents a lady
from above the Arctic Circle dressed in a
''fancy'' parka.

Materials: Carved and painted birch
head, wolverine tail hair, twisted caribou
sinew hair ties; Arctic ground squirrel
parka with pieced calf skin ''fancy
work,'' wolverine head fringe and alder
bark-dyed seal skin trim, land otter tail
cuffs, wolverine chin fur dangles, seed
bead trim, outer ruff of badger mane
and coyote chin fur, inner ruff of
wolverine forehead fur and bleached
caribou skin; body and pants are seal
skin, mittens are spotted seal belly.
Mukluks are summer barren ground
caribou legs with land otter belly uppers
edged at the top with alder bark-dyed

seal skin and joined to caribou skin soles
with strip of alder bark-dyed caribou
skin; strings are winter-bleached seal
skin. The doll is sewn entirely with
twisted caribou sinew.

Eskimo Dolls

by Susan W. Fair

Origins

The art of making dolls has been practiced by Alaskan Eskimos for at least two thousand years. Carved wood and ivory human figurines, for the most part highly stylized and artistic, are the earliest doll prototypes. They lay buried in ancient frozen village and camp sites over a wide area of coastal Alaska until their relatively recent excavation by archaeologists seeking to know more about the people who made and used them, and by those who dig them up for sale as art objects for a lucrative, if surreptitious market.

Prehistoric Eskimo art underwent several major stylistic transitions which can be documented through the artifacts these early cultures left behind. These artifacts comprise a body of artistry that ranks prehistoric Alaskan Eskimo carvers among the great creators of art in the world. Carved ivory dolls comprise a significant portion of these artifacts, and a few of the features common to modern Eskimo dolls can be seen in these earlier, more stylized prototypes.

Figurines of the Okvik culture (300 B.C.) constitute the oldest, most classic doll-form. The Okvik culture inhabited St. Lawrence Island, the Punuk Islands, and a few other locations in Siberia and Alaska, but the materials they left behind are best known from the Punuk Islands site. Forty-five doll figurines are cited in a collection made on the Punuk Islands in the 1930's (Collins:1973:4), but that figure has surely made a dramatic increase by this time, since the trade in artifacts, particularly those with human or animal form, has become lucrative.

Okvik dolls were carved of walrus ivory (fig. 1). Their heads are generally large in relation to a body which often has no arms or legs. They are characterized by a facial structure which is elegant and carefully sculpted, with a brow ridge and nose structure that can still be seen in nearly identical form on many post-contact twentieth century wood-faced dolls. Features of this same face type can be traced from prehistoric to contemporary times and are today exemplified in the work of dollmaker Susie Brown of Eek, whose wood-faced family group is represented in the exhibit.

Engraved tattoo marks are also common to Okvik doll faces, highlighting a cultural practice which was in vogue as recently as the early twentieth century.

Anchorage Historical and Fine Arts Museum

Fig. 1. *Ivory Okvik figure (5" high) said to come from the Punuk Islands, is now in the collection of the Anchorage Historical and Fine Arts Museum. Okvik figures, characterized by classic, elegant faces, are some of the earliest Eskimo "dolls."*

One project dollmaker, Josephine Ungott of Gambell, has tattoos on her face and hands, as do several of the older St. Lawrence Island women, and tattoos can be seen etched on the "Favorite Daughter" doll made by Annie Alowa of Savoonga.

Many Okvik figurines are headless. Conversely, many isolated Okvik doll heads can be found which cannot be matched to a corresponding body, indicating that the separation of the two was accidental (as might happen in children's play), or that if done intentionally, the pieces were disposed of in separate locations. In *Eskimo Art*, Vol. 1, Dorothy Jean Ray writes that a custom existed on St. Lawrence Island of breaking dolls at a special site as part of a ritual associated with the death of a child and that this practice was still common in the late 1920's (1977:10). Jack Herman Ningealook, seventy-eight year old elder from Shishmaref, in talking about dolls he remembers from his childhood, said that "the shamen or medicine men were the only ones that had dolls. They used them as charms; if the medicine man dies, then they cut off the head of the doll. That's why when there's people find some without heads that meant the medicine man died—they take the head off."* Since headless ivory dolls are numerous, it seems unlikely that this mutilation was accidental, and it is probable that dolls were commonly used for these ritualistic or ceremonial purposes from prehistoric times into the twentieth century.

Carved doll figurines are present during several later cultural periods after Okvik, including Old Bering Sea (Okvik is sometimes regarded as a closely related phase of this larger culture), Punuk (900 A.D.), and Thule (500-1000 A.D.), but they are completely absent from the highly artistic, partially contemporary Ipiutak culture at Point Hope (350 A.D.).

These early figurines may well have been dressed, possibly for use as playthings. The bodies of dolls from Okvik and later periods, in contrast to the elegant carefully carved faces, are often rudimentary. Many of the bodies are no more than a stubby wedge whose only grace lies in the engraved lines that sometimes cover it. These lines appear to represent clothing, tattooing, or sexual features, sometimes in very stylized form.

*All quotes and information from dollmakers are from interviews conducted between March - May, 1982, by Susan W. Fair and Suzi Jones. The audio recordings and the transcriptions and translations of these interviews are being deposited in the Arctic and Polar Regions Collection of the Rasmuson Library at the University of Alaska, Fairbanks. Interviews were conducted in an individual's first language when possible, with the assistance of local interpreters.

It is the lack of limbs that is the most interesting feature in comparing older doll figurines with modern Eskimo dolls. Simple wedge-shaped shoulders and bodies with more realistic, carved wooden heads are citied by Wendell Oswalt as having been recovered from archaeological sites near Hooper Bay and referred to as dolls. The grave of a child excavated by Oswalt near the mouth of the Yukon river yielded thirteen such dolls (1952:71). This find corresponds to the doll sets, or families, described by several villagers in Southwest Alaska as common children's playthings in the early part of the century, and several dolls in this exhibit are manufactured along this same principle. Reindeer horn dolls from Shishmaref always lacked carved arms; their phantom arms exist only in the stuffed arms of their parkas. The dolls with carved wood heads by dollmakers Susie Brown, Eva Heffle, and Dolly Spencer have only abbreviated torsos or necks which are attached to cloth bodies, as do the ivory headed dolls made by Savoonga dollmakers Annie Alowa and the Kingeekuks.

One feature of early dolls which seems to indicate that at least some were made to be clothed and possibly played with is the presence of a deep groove which encircles the head and face of some dolls. Five of the carved ivory dolls pictured in Dorothy Jean Ray's *Aleut and Eskimo Art* (p. 145) have such grooves behind their faces. One has blue string in the groove and around the doll's neck. All of these figurines were collected by E.W. Nelson in what are now the villages of Pilot Village and Marshall between 1878-1881 (Ray:1981:145). Other dolls with grooved heads were excavated by Wendell Oswalt in Hooper Bay (1952:70) and Anne Shinkwin at Point Hope (1977:184), and many more are likely to exist.

In recent years I have seen old dolls with such grooves excavated by villagers in Shishmaref. Local speculation was that the groove was designed to facilitate hanging the piece as a pendant. More recently, I examined a relatively new doll in the collection of Donna Hobson of Anchorage, which had a similar groove encircling its face (fig. 2). The doll has a carefully carved stained and painted wood face with features reminiscent of Okvik. It was made by an unknown dollmaker from somewhere in the Bethel region within the last ten years, and the purpose of the face groove is to attach both the cloth stuffed body and parka hood to its face.

Rob Stapleton

Fig. 2. *This doll, made in a southwest Alaska village in the 1970's, has a groove around the perimeter of its wood face, where the doll's soft, cloth head is attached. The technique of construction appears to date back to early doll figures.*

Today's Eskimo Dolls

Whether the small human figurines excavated at archeological sites were made as ceremonial objects, amulets, or children's toys will undoubtedly remain a question for researchers in years to come. Most researchers use the term *figurine* when referring to such objects in scholarly studies; however, the term *doll* is often applied to these same objects in popular publications and in everyday conversation. Eskimo villagers, when speaking in English, refer to both the ancient figures and to contemporary works like those in this exhibit as *dolls*. At the present time, our research into the Native language terms for old figures and contemporary pieces does, in some cases, suggest that different terms are used, but such linguistic research is still in its preliminary stages and more information will be necessary before we can offer any conclusions.

Most readers of this catalog probably use the term *doll* to refer to children's toys, and most dolls in this exhibit would delight any child, but none were intended as playthings. Each was made as a craft (or art) object for sale to collectors, museums, tourists, or visitors to villages. There has, however, been a tradition of making dolls for children's toys, especially in southwest Alaska as recently as two generations ago, and in a very few instances, still today. But by and large,

today's young Eskimo girls play with commercially manufactured dolls.

Eskimo dolls, as they are made today, and presented here, are craft items which have been made according to local cultural traditions and aesthetics, especially in carving and skin sewing. The dolls are usually dressed in highly traditional clothing (often historic), and they are crafted mainly from materials derived from the local subsistence way of life. Of course, there are exceptions, and today all dollmakers avail themselves of "western" materials to some extent, but in most cases the materials and ideas resulting from contact with white culture have been adapted on Eskimo cultural terms, and the dollmaking process and the dolls themselves are identifiably Eskimo. In sum, the dollmakers, their aesthetics, the materials (and preparation of the materials), the methods of carving and sewing, the style of the dolls' clothing, hair, and ornamentation are Eskimo. The consumer is frequently non-Eskimo.

Although I have been using the general term, *Eskimo*, it should be pointed out that this exhibit features individuals from three related but distinct Eskimo linguistic/cultural groups in Alaska: Inupiaq, Central Yup'ik, and St. Lawrence Island Yup'ik. Within the Yup'ik region, residents of Chevak speak a dialect called Cup'ik, and they refer to themselves, their language and their culture as Cup'ik rather than the more general term, Yup'ik.

The dolls in this exhibit can be identified not only as Eskimo, but more specifically as Inupiaq, Yup'ik, or Siberian Yup'ik, and within these categories, even further by village, and in many cases by individual dollmaker. Although much traditional or tribal art, including Eskimo dolls, is sold, displayed, and written about is if most artists were "anonymous," this is an unsatisfactory approach to such art. For while it is true that *cultural* features are important and often pre-eminent in traditional arts, the style of the *individual* artist is almost always also discernible and important to any real understanding of the art. One need only look at Dolly Spencer's doll to realize that the traditional art does not fall into some deep well of sameness and convention that renders the individual artist anonymous, thus powerless. Spencer's dolls are all meticulous, highly recognizable portraits (fig. 3) which could only be confused with the work of one other dollmaker, her predecessor Ethel Washington of Kotzebue, and this probably only to the non-Native eye. Any dolls encountered in the research for this project which are referred to as ''anonymous'' only means that **I** don't know who made them. If the dolls, even the older ones that have been in the museums or private collections, unidentified for forty or fifty years, were to be taken to a few most logical villages for identification, the makers would be identified surely and quickly, even if they were no longer living. I once took a tiny carved ivory button of very fine quality with me on a trip to Gambell to see if I could find out who carved it. The button had been collected by a teacher who lived on St. Lawrence Island in the thirties. I showed it to Tom Iworrigan, a seventy-year-old carver whose style was somewhat similar (Tom is now deceased), who said with delight that he had made the button himself fifty years ago, and examined it as though putting his current work to test.

Economics of Dollmaking

Each of the dollmakers represented in the exhibit makes dolls specifically to sell, and almost all began their dollmaking careers to supplement family income. Some are the only wage earners in their family. Joesphine Ungott, seventy-six-year-old dollmaker from Gambell, first began making dolls in the 1920's in the style of her mentor and relative, Flora Tungiyan, because traders and sailors coming to the island by boat requested them. Margaret Ahlalook of Wainwright originally began dollmaking ''so she could buy some groceries,'' as did Anaktuvuk's Susie Paneak, who ''wanted money, too'' because she had no job. Mary Nash of Chevak began making dolls in 1957 and used the money from their sale to purchase family Christmas presents, while Martina Oscar of Bethel says that she started making dolls in 1953 ''to make a few bucks.'' Eva Heffle of North Pole is perhaps the only dollmaker represented here who did not begin dollmaking intending to sell the finished product. Her career

began more as an accidental offshoot of sewing, and she describes herself as being ''thrilled'' when she sold her first doll in Seattle in the early 1960's. While Heffle probably earns substantial income now from sales of her various dolls, she still considers dollmaking a hobby, not a profession, and says she simply likes doing it. Maggie Komonaseak of Wales, whose husband Silas is an accomplished ivory carver, depends on the dolls to supplement family income although she also works as a cook at the school: ''It comes in pretty handy sometimes when I'm flat broke, and I get somebody to come around and buy a doll, or someone send a check or money order. It helps me, although I'm working, you know, it helps. . . .''

Aesthetics

The fact that these eighteen dollmakers manufacture dolls for sale has not interfered with their personal standards of craftsmanship, however. It is important to sew well, and for most women this means that the stitches must be meticulous and close together. According to Gudmund Hatt's classic monograph on Arctic clothing, an overcast stitch is most commonly used so that seams will not press against the body (1962:22). Giffen, quoting Stefansson and Jenness, states tha the reason for meticulous stitchery is that the ''seams of the Eskimo housewife must be waterproof, and in turning out the necessary garments she sometimes works far into the night'' (1930:34). The quality of skin resulting from the tanning procedure is another criterion of talent among Eskimo women. For instance, the whiteness of winter-bleached seal skin or seal intestine, widely used in dollmaking, is very important. The skin can yellow perceptibly if the tanner is not patient and careful. Josephine Ungott of Gambell describes the process, starting from the point where the hunters in the family have brought home a bearded seal and the intestine has been removed: ''I take the outer skin off, then I turn them (the intestines) inside out and use the scraper to scrape the inside skin off. After that I put them in water. Day after day I change the water until the water is clear. When the water isn't cloudy any more, I inflate them, take them outside and freeze them dry. This is done only in winter when it is real cold. Only cold air dries them nice and white.'' In addition to the quality of the materials used and the fineness of the stitching, other signs of craftsmanship important to

Fig. 3. *A close-up of a Dolly Spencer doll shows how life-like the carved birch face is and how much attention to realistic detail is involved in the creation of one of Spencer's dolls.*

Chris Arend

dollmakers include the carving, the accuracy of the clothing style, and the facial expressions, especially on dolls with carved faces.

Alaskan Dollmakers

Dollmakers are not, as a group, easily categorized. Doll manufacture is primarily, but not exclusively, the art of women. Elliot Olanna is the only male dollmaker featured in this exhibit, and the inclusion of his sculptural whalebone figures as dolls may be stretching the definition to its limits. Among Shishmaref whalebone sculptors, however, Olanna's family figures rank with the most realistic, while the work of other carvers runs a gamut of abstraction of the human form, Olanna's whalebone dolls are never clothed. On the other hand, horn dolls are always clothed, and Emma Olanna makes the clothing for the horn dolls while Elliot carves the bodies. This sort of collaboration is typical among dollmakers in Shishmaref unless special circumstances exist. Dollmakers who are widows often carve doll bodies themselves, as do women whose husbands are too busy or who are poor carvers.

Other known male dollmakers include Laurie Kingik of Point Hope, whose model umiaks filled with miniature hunters are masterpieces. Sam Fox, an accomplished mask maker and carver from Dillingham, is also a dollmaker, and there are reports of at least two men in Kivalina who make dolls.

Men often have roles in dollmaking other than carving doll bodies. Margaret Ahlalook's late husband made the wood and ivory harpoons for her hunter dolls until his death in 1981. Now she carves the miniatures herself, saying that it is the most laborious, time-consuming part of her dollmaking. Maggie Komonaseak of Wales says she doesn't make dolls at all if her husband Silas doesn't carve the faces, but her mother, Carrie Weyapuk, carves her own doll faces. Maggie also adds that her husband and one of her sons occasionally help sew doll clothing for her, Silas doing so only "when he's bored or tired of carving." More than half of the dollmakers interviewed make their dolls with no help, although some like Susie Paneak and Margaret Ahlalook, do so only because their husbands are no longer living. For others, dollmaking is a collaborative effort, though it is the woman who is generally given credit for the finished

product. Floyd and Amelia Kingeekuk of Savoonga are an exception, adopting a "we both" approach when asked which one is the dollmaker. In their case, it is clear that their dolls would not be made at all without the dedicated participation of both partners. In general, dollmaking is primarily a female activity, and this can be traced to traditional Eskimo male-female roles. Naomi Giffen in *The Roles of Men and Women in Eskimo Culture,* writes that women's activities include "the use of the mouth and teeth of the housewife in the performance of her daily tasks, namely, in the dressing of skins, the softening of boot soles, tearing of sinew thread . . ."and many more (1930:79).

Can any Eskimo woman make a doll? Many villagers seem to think so, although there are skinsewers in every village who do not make them. Dollmakers seem to proliferate when one or several women in a village have begun making dolls that are very salable, as well as in villages where there is a long-standing, firm, dollmaking tradition, such as in Wales, Shishmaref, and Chevak. Dollmaker Annie Alowa says that in Savoonga there are "lots of ladies who do nice work," although few of them make dolls. Anna Pootoogooluk of Shishmaref, who is an excellent, very inventive sewer, says that she has never tried to make dolls "even though it looks easy." Many dollmakers spoke of the difficulties involved in sewing mukluks and mittens in miniature, and it may be a preference for small scale that leads some sewers to make dolls while others choose not to.

Learning the Art

Dollmaking is almost always learned by watching. Generally, the artists included in this exhibit observed their mothers and then tried dollmaking on their own, sometimes with mixed results. Susie Brown of Eek remembers her first doll with some humor: "the faces were good, but I made the little shoes too big . . . this guy that wanted to buy some didn't want to buy them 'cause the feet were too big." Emma Olanna recalls that she "just learned how to. When I first start . . . learn how to decide what to do (with) myself. Nobody taught me." Annie Alowa was encouraged by her mother, Olga Akeya, to try dollmaking alone as well, so she "just tried and tried, and cut out everything; made patterns myself." Maggie Komonaseak of Wales had a little more help, originally

using her mother's patterns and depending on her sewing tips, as did other village women "that didn't have a mom . . . (they would) go to my mom and let her show how to make seal skin pants or parka." Some of her mother's advice would have seemed harsh to a non-Native girl who expected to be taught: "She used to tell me to learn instead of let her do them for me, by her for me. Said that's the only way you learn, by doing . . . Like the first pair of hunting mukluks I made, she wouldn't help me with them. I felt like crying. She want me to learn." Some dollmakers, including Maggie and her mother, are very willing to share their skills and say that they wish village women who need help with their sewing would ask for patterns or assistance, but they rarely do.

Knowledge of who is an excellent skinsewer or dollmaker in a village does exist among Eskimo women, though explicit, stated comparisons are rare. There is no sense of competition with the Western aura of winning or losing, but rather a quiet, private acknowledgement of the skills of others. Anthropoligist Sarkis Atamian, in writing about mask making in the village of Anaktuvuk Pass, suggests that there is a strong social stigma placed on overt competition among Eskimo groups which "restrains the individual from flaunting his superiority, or abusing it" (1966:1344), and Dorothy Jean Ray reaffirms this, saying that a "good carver has his high standards, but he will never tell another person that he, himself, is a good carver, or that an object he made is a fine piece" (1961:153).

This was born out in our interviews with dollmakers and others. Jack Herman Nigealook, Shishmaref elder, says that an ideal reindeer horn doll must look "exactly like a human being and [be] well dressed," and he goes on to tell of a contest staged in the early 1920's between himself, Harry Olanna of Brevig Mission, and several other people to see who could make the "best-looking" horn doll. (The reindeer horn doll was virtually a brand new invention at that time.) It was a contest without a winner. Ningealook states only that the participants "would compare among themselves before they go and sell it," but he can remember to this day whose dolls were the best looking ones. An excerpt from our interview with Amelia Kingeekuk and interpreter, George Noongwook, is interesting for what it reveals about attitudes toward modesty and pride:

Interviewer: Is it [dollmaking] competitive?

G. Noongwook: Not out right in front. No, you don't go out and say it. There's competition, but subtly.

Interviewer: Has that always been true?

G. Noongwook: No. No, I think that a lot of our people were brought up not to be boastful of their work.

Interviewer: But wasn't it always obvious—

G. Noongwook: It was obvious—

Interviewer: —that a certain person was an excellent seamstress?

G. Noongwook: Oh yes. Those were some of the ideal characteristics of a woman—you have to be able to be a good sewer so you can provide for the clothing of your family once you become married. That was one of the qualities men looked for . . . .

A. Kingeekuk: I don't want to be perfect. My kids always say, don't try to be perfect—I mean for making things to be proud of.

Interviewer: They say "do" or "don't"?

A Kingeekuk: They *don't* want me to be proud of my things.

Interviewer: Why not?

A Kingeekuk: I'm not.

Interviewer: Do you want to be proud of them? You are proud of them aren't you?

G. Noongwook: (unclear)—not to brag, but let others recognize your good characteristics . . . it's always better to have somebody recognize your good qualities, your good characteristics by other people . . . When you compare it to western man where you try to put your best foot forward and you want to be your very best when you're presenting yourself, especially for a job interview or something—acccording to our traditions and values, that's not real good for someone to come right out and say that you're the very best in this field.

Dollmakers within their own villages may be able to name the other women who are producing dolls but are unlikely to have seen the dolls unless they have been displayed for sale in the village store. In part, this is a result of a Native doll art market in which the consumer is usually from outside the village, and most dolls are mailed out to buyers immediately upon completion. This may also be a consequence of some intentional secrecy among artists, especially since there is a very wide range in the pricing of dolls, or it may simply reflect a reticence on the part of villagers to boldly or impolitely ask to see the work of other artists unless an appropriate time presents itself. Although generally unaware of other dollmakers, in some cases, artists and their families proved very helpful in pointing out how a particular style might have evolved, and some even acknowledge copying a particular doll style from the artist who originated it. Occasionally, copying seemed to be resented when it took place outside the family group; however, because the dolls never look exactly alike anyway, *individual interpretation of a style* might be a more appropriate term than copying.

Dolls for Ceremony and Magic

As noted earlier, there appear to be many types of Eskimo figurines which are referred to as dolls. Some of these were made for ceremonial, magic, or shamanistic purposes, while others were simply toys. Some of the ceremonial pieces were elaborate, jointed dolls or puppets according to reports of missionaries and explorers in the nineteenth century. One such appealing puppet is pictured in *Aleut and Eskimo Art* (Ray:1981:188), and is labeled a shaman's hand puppet. It is composed of a fox pup skin bag and has a sly, rather seductive doll-like face made of stained wood. Ray notes that although it is difficult to ascertain which of the older dolls were made as toys and which as amulets, "in general most of the human figurines made of ivory were dolls and those of wood were charms and fetishes" (1977:10). Hans Himmelheber, who is cited in Ray's *Aleut and Eskimo Art*, apparently collected many carved ivory human and animal figurines north of Norton Sound in 1936, and he has reported that these objects were made and sold by shamans in order to bring good hunting to their purchasers, while people in the Kuskokwim region did not have such charms at that time, however, and most could not remember seeing anything like them (Ray:1981:21). The use of carved figurines as charms is a custom seemingly universal among Eskimos. Meldgaard, in *Eskimo Sculpture*, attributes to an old East-Greenlander a beautiful passage regarding the carving of dwarf willows into dolls which were then fastened inside the parka hood of young boys. The charm was said not only to "make a boy grow fast, (like a willow), but will give him a strong back so that he can walk through life erect and fearless" (1960:7). In the past a "doll festival" existed on the lower Yukon and extended as far upriver as Anvik, where it had been adopted by Athabaskans. This year, a Grayling resident told me that the "Doll Dance" was practiced in a nearby village sometime before 1954, and the dolls were used for divining the future. E.W. Nelson documented aspects of the festival in detail in the late nineteenth century, noting that the center of attention during various ceremonies in the kashim was a wooden doll, which was wrapped in birchbark and hung in a tree at a secret spot for the rest of the year. The shaman fed deer fat or dry fish to the doll during its isolation and consulted it "to ascertain what success will attend the season's hunting or fishing" (Nelson:1899:494).

Other information collected by Nelson in the lower Yukon attributes to a carved wooden doll the origin of winds, the custom of wearing masks, and perhaps even the origins of dollmaking itself in this region. This legend may also be related to the fairly recent beliefs and customs in southwest Alaska which associate dolls with weather. Several older dollmakes in southwest Alaska said that as young girls they did not play with dolls in the winter because it was believed that playing with dolls out of season would result in either bad weather or unending winter.

Origin of Winds
(From the lower Yukon)

In a village on the lower Yukon lived a man and his wife who had no children. After a long time the woman spoke to her husband one day and said, "I can not understand why we have no children; can you?" To which the husband replied that he could not. She then told her husband to go on the tundra to a solitary tree that grew there and bring back a part of its trunk and make a doll from it. The man went out of the house and saw a long track of bright light, like that made by the moon shining on the snow, leading off across the tundra in the direction he must take. Along this path of light he traveled far away until he saw before him a beautiful object shining in the bright light. Going up to it, he found that it was the tree for which he came in search. The tree was small, so he took his hunting knife, cut off a part of its trunk and carried the fragment home.

When he returned he sat down and carved from the wood an image of a small boy, for which his wife made a couple of suits of fur clothing in which she dressed it. Directed by his wife, the man then carved a set of toy dishes from the wood, but said he could see no use for all this trouble, as it would make them no better off than they were before. To this his wife replied that before they had nothing but themselves to talk about, but the doll would give them amusement and a subject of conversation. She then deposited the doll in the place of honor on the bench opposite the entrance, with the toy dishes full of food and water before it.

When the couple had gone to bed that night and the room was very dark they heard several low whistling sounds. The woman shook her husband, saying, "Do you hear that? It was the doll;" to which he agreed. They got up at once, and, making a light, saw that the doll had eaten the food and drank the water, and they could see its eyes move. The woman caught it up with delight and fondled and played with it for a long time. When she became tired it was put back on the bench and they went to bed again.

In the morning, when the couple got up, they found the doll was gone. They looked for it about the house, but could find no trace of it, and, going outside, found its tracks leading away from the door. These tracks passed from the door along the bank of a small creek until a little outside the village, where they ended, as the doll had walked from this place on the path of light upon which the man had gone to find the tree.

The man and his wife followed no farther but went home. Doll had traveled on along the bright path until he came to the edge of day, where the sky comes down to the earth and walls in the light. Close to where he was, in the east, he saw a gut-skin fastened over the hole in the sky wall, which was bulging inward apparently owing to some strong force on the other side. The doll stopped and said, "It is very quiet in here. I think a

little wind will make it better." So he drew his knife and cut the cover loose about the edge of the hole, and a strong wind blew through, every now and then bringing with it a live reindeer. Looking through the hole, Doll say beyond the wall another world like earth. He drew the cover over the hole again and bade the wind not to blow too hard, but he said "Sometimes blow hard, sometimes light, and sometimes do not blow at all."

Then he walked along the sky wall until he came to another opening at the southeast, which was covered, and the covering pressed inward like the first. When he cut this cover loose the force of the gale swept in, bringing reindeer, trees, and bushes. Closing the hole again, he bade it do as he had told the first one, and passed on. In a short time he came to a hole in the south, and when the cover was cut a hot wind came rushing in accompanied by rain and the spray from the great sea lying beyond the sky hole on that side.

Doll closed this opening and instructed it as before, and passed on to the west. There he saw another opening, and as soon as the cover was cut the wind brought in a heavy rainstorm, with sleet and spray, from the ocean. This opening was also closed, with the same instruction, and he passed on to the northwest, where he found another opening. When the cover to this was cut away a blast of cold wind came rushing in, bringing in snow and ice, so that he was chilled to the bone and half frozen, and he hastened to close it, as he had the others.

Again he went along the sky wall to the north, the cold becoming so great that he was obligated to leave it and make a circuit, going back to it where he saw the opening. There the cold was so intense that he hesitated for some time, but finally cut the cover away. At once a fearful blast rushed in, carrying great masses of snow and ice, strewing it all over the earth plain. He closed the hole very quickly, and having admonished it as usual, traveled on until he came to the middle of the earth plain.

When he reached there he looked up and saw the sky arching overhead, supported by long, slender poles, arranged like those of a conical lodge, but made of some beautiful material unknown to him. Turning again, he traveled far away, until he reached the village whence he had started. There he circled once completely around the place, and

then entered one after the other of the houses, going to his own home last of all. This he did that the people should become his friends, and care for him in case his parents should die.

After this Doll lived in the village for a very long time. When his foster parents died he was taken by other people, and so lived for many generations, until finally he died. From him people learned the custom of wearing masks, and since his death parents have been accustomed to make dolls for their children in imitation of the people who made the one of which I have told.

(Nelson:1899:497-99).

Wood doll figurines were used, at least on St. Lawrence Island, in ceremonies connected with whaling. When doing research on the island, Otto Geist learned that a ceremony was conducted by whaling captains who burned the dolls when it was over. Geist also noted that "carved figures of this kind are now "fed" with blubber and meat during certain ceremonies" (Geist and Rainey:1936:123). Nelson Alowa of Savoonga remembers hearing about the dolls: "They have a hole just like a mouth . . . They feed with a little seal blubber, grease, sour grease; they put in the mouth just like a human. Before they sing they took a doll — that's why I heard the story 'way back in old custom."

Another legend about dolls comes from Hooper Bay. According to the legend, Ooloo, the daughter of Netchek, was forbidden to marry the young man of her choice, and so refused to marry at all. Eventually, her father no longer wished to hunt for her, and became so angry that he threw a piece of blubber at her, saying, "Then you can marry this blubber." Ooloo carved a boy doll from the frozen blubber and clothed it in doll clothing she made herself. She pretended that the doll was real, and when she turned her back, a handsome young man took the blubber doll's place. She married the young man. He was a good hunter and fine husband, but with the warmth of spring, Blubber Boy became weak and finally melted away into the floor of his kayak. Ooloo was not disturbed by this, for she knew that when winter came "she could make Blubber Boy again with her ivory picture knife. Then she could dress him in the doll clothes and wish him back to her" (Gillham:1955:107-110).

51

Toy Dolls

No dolls made for the purposes of ceremony or magic were included in the exhibit because, as far as we know, none are currently being made. Neither was a doll made specifically as a toy included. Although the great majority of contemporary Eskimo dolls are made for sale to the collector or for the tourist trade, dolls made as playthings for Eskimo girls are still being produced in some villages. They have not been included here because they are made to be cuddled and touched and generally do not have the visual appeal of their more artistic cousins represented here. Kathy Schwartz, formerly an art teacher in both Kivalina and Selawik, reports that at least two Kivalina sewers still make dolls for play. These dolls, approximately ten inches tall, have simply carved wood or whalebone faces and are generally wearing plain Arctic ground squirrel parkas. Schwartz reports having seen Kivalina girls sleeping with such dolls as recently as 1979. This tradition of making dolls for play may very well be carried forward, at least in Kivalina, for dollmaker Nellie Swan has taught workshops in the high school instructing young women in the construction of such dolls. Kivalina is the only northern village contacted where the present production of dolls as toys could be confirmed.

On St. Lawrence Island, one Savoonga dollmaker, Flora Imergan, had much to say about the function of dolls when she was a young girl (fig. 4). Flora, who is now sixty-eight, began to learn carving at the age of thirteen by watching her grandfather, *Nemayaq*, who carved at their homes in Gambell and Camp Collier. Pioneer Alaskan archaeologist Otto Geist visited *Nemayaq* in 1927, describing him as "a brother of the strongest shaman on the island, and carver of the many dolls, idols, fetishes and ornamented household utensils . . . found in many of the island homes." (Geist and Rainey:1936:34). According to Geist, he left the camp laden with gifts, and it is likely that he collected some of *Namayaq's* wooden dolls at that time. Flora, who would have been a teenager at the time, remembers saving some of her grandfather's dolls and selling them to Geist in Camp Collier sometime around 1930.

Imergan describes the dolls as being of all varieties, including "mothers breastfeeding dolls, legs crossed, all different designs." There are at least fifteen dolls in the collection at the Univer-

Fig. 4. *Flora Imergan, Savoonga, provided information on how dolls were made and used when she was a girl. Her father,* Nemayaq, *was a noted carver and many of his works are in the University Museum in Fairbanks.*

sity of Alaska Museum which can probably be accurately attributed to *Nemayaq* (fig. 5). In addition to the dolls described from memory by Flora Imergan, there are skillfully carved driftwood figures of women giving birth, carrying children, and feeding them, as well as many other poses. Geist reported that some of the mother and child figurines were carved as "fertility figures" by shamans who "prescribed them for use as charms by barren women who wished to have children" (Van Stone:1953:20).

Young Flora did not play with the wooden dolls made by her grandfather, but *Nemayaq* did make other dolls for her to play with. One such doll had a

leather body with "picks" attached at the shoulders, giving the upper limbs free movement. Flora also had play dolls that she describes as having been "made by white men with clay heads and hands." These were probably bisque or porcelain dolls brought in by whalers and traders. She says the *Nemayaq* copied these dolls, apparently substituting one of his for the fragile china doll that Flora played with.

She also states that her mother, *Quyaalaq*, made dolls with driftwood faces, as well as figures with ivory hands and carved ivory full-round heads. Some of the these dolls were baby dolls, but it is likely that the ones with ivory heads were not. It is possible that *Quyaalaq* may have been the originator of the dolls with ivory head and hands that come from Savoonga and are represented here in the works of Annie Alowa and the Kingeekuks. Jeanette Noongwook, a Savoonga elder who recently died, also made this type of doll, as do several other contemporary Savoonga women.

Baby dolls made as toys were used primarily in the island communities of

University of Alaska Museum, Fairbanks

Fig. 5. *This figure is one of* Nemayaq's *carvings.*

Fig. 6. *This illustration of a Chukchi doll appeared in 1882 in Nordenskiold's* Voyage of the Vega. *Baby dolls similar to this are still made by St. Lawrence Island women.*

the Bering Sea and possibly at times on the mainland. Several St. Lawrence Island women still make baby dolls in the traditional style, including Caroline Penayah (who made a different Siberian Yup'ik doll for the exhibit); Annie Alowa; and the Omwari family, which includes Hazel, her fifty-five-year-old daughter Pansy, and a younger daughter. All three women make baby dolls. (Pansy was originally commissioned to make a baby doll for the exhibit, but was unable to complete the piece because of her mother's failing health.)

Most baby dolls of recent manufacture are simply made, with stuffed cloth bodies, bleached seal skin faces, and embroidered features. They are dressed in clothing referred to by Siberian Yup'ik women as "buntings" or *qallevak.* Baby doll clothing replicates clothing sewn for Eskimo infants, and Caroline Penayah says that children were dressed in buntings until they began to walk. This style is said by scholars to have Northeast Asian origins (fig. 6). Buntings are made of heavy cloth or skin (often reindeer fawnskin), and consist of two identical snowsuit halves seamed down the center front and back, a hood, and an opening at the crotch designed for the insertion and removal of Sphagnum moss diapers (Nordenskiold: 1882:298). When we visted Savoonga dollmaker Annie Alowa, she showed us a full-size blue velveteen bunting she had made for one of her grand-daughters. The most conspicuous feature of this bunting is a very ornate belt comprised of assorted baby gifts, including the old wedding rings of family members, bells, and trade beads. The same asemblage of materials also hangs from sleeve cuffs. Annie says the the noisy ornaments are there to alert anyone to the baby's presence, and that the object hanging from the sleeves assisted a mother in packing a child.

Further evidence that the baby doll toy as well as bunting style infant clothing is of Siberian origin comes from several residents of Northwest Alaska. Annie Alowa had such a doll when she was young, and her husband Nelson relates seeing girls playing outside with similar dolls when he visited Siberia in the 1930's. He described the dolls as being "just like a baby," clothed in fawnskins with heads of bleached white seal skin. He says that they were "big just like a one year old."

Helen Okpealuk, a sixty-six-year-old dollmaker who moved from Little

Diomede to Wales in 1956, recalls seeing a slightly different doll brought from Siberia sometime during the 1920's to Little Diomede. The young Siberian girl who owned the doll was said to be the survivor of a pair of twins. She had accompanied her aunt to the island and was packing a large doll about eighteen inches tall on her back. Okpealuk recalls being told that the doll had been made as a replacement playmate for the girl's lost twin. She did not see the doll's face, but remembers that it was wearing adult female clothing and waterproof springtime mukluks with bearded seal skin tops. Helen does not remember seeing any Little Diomede children playing with homemade dolls during that era.

Eskimo play dolls of assorted materials are recorded in literature, along with toys such as miniature sleds, string buzzers, tops made for spinning, small boats and model hunting equipment for boys. Weasels, stuffed and skinned, with beaded eyes, are said to have been occasionally substituted for dolls (Voss:1970:20). Today, in Chevak, Margaret Slats makes hunter dolls holding small stuffed weasels or squirrels to represent the hunters' game. Another type of doll that uses animal parts may be a recent invention; some dolls from the Yukon delta have rodent paws or crab claws as occasional substitutes for hands.

Rob Stapleton

Fig. 7. *Liz Ali, Bethel, holds a doll made for her by her grandmother, Marie Nichols, who lives in Kasigluk. This is the type of miniature doll which was made for children to play with in Yup'ik villages. These dolls are seldom made nowadays.*

Cloth stuffed rag dolls are now rare, but were once used as playthings. Susie Brown of Eek played with rag dolls when she was young.

The lower jawbone of a walrus was also used extensively as a play doll by girls on St. Lawrence Island. Judy Pelowook and Caroline Penayah, both of Savoogna, recounted playing with these jawbone dolls, wrapping clothing around them and carrying them in a pack or straddling a shoulder. Pelowook says that such dolls were used in "almost every household" at one time. Theresa Rookook Kava, also a Savoonga resident, did not play with walrus jawbone dolls, but recalls using miniature wood and ivory figures, carved by her father and grandfather during the 1940's. Most of her miniature dolls were one to two inches tall.

Ethnographers often ascribe to Eskimo toy dolls the function of instructive models, highlighting for Eskimo girls "those activities of domestic life which they would be called on to practice all of their adult lives" (Anderson and Eels:1935:69). While it is true that such playful activities such as hunting mice with miniature bows and arrows or feeding and clothing dolls prepare children for adult responsibilities, it should not be forgotten that "playing house" was also fun.

In Southwest Alaska most dollmakers interviewed said that dolls are not made as toys at the present time; however, almost all the women interviewed had fresh memories of playing with dolls and recounted many stories about them (fig. 7). Dollmaker Helen H. Smith of Hooper Bay and her sisters Natalia Smith and Neva Rivers vividly remember playing with dolls when they were children. However, strict taboos governed the use of dolls when the three sisters grew up, and if the rules were ignored, hardship could come not only to the girls but to the entire village. The sisters said that they had families of dolls for which they made little houses, and that their dolls had "everything—Eskimo things . . . and they got their own beddings, and after we play with them, we wrap them up and tie them up and put them in a bundle until we're going to play again. But in wintertime they used to store them away. We never used to use them in summertime until the cranes come . . . .

"We have a story too. Everything used to be strict. We're not supposed to play

ball in wintertime or play with our dolls. That's the way we used to believe then. They used to tell us." [Interviewer: "What was the story about?"] "Like if we play with our dolls before the crane comes, or if we take them out, we would have a punishment for it. We would have real long winter. They will let us freeze, and hang us up and freeze us for punishment. That thing, we used to believe it."

Helen Smith said that the dolls were put away at the end of summer, "when it's freezing, when the snow comes, when the first snow comes." These dolls were made of rags, wood or ivory, and they were dressed in cloth scraps by the girls. Girls played with dolls until their first monthly periods: "When the girl have her first monthly period, that's the time she don't keep her things. She give them away." Helen noted that her older sister was "kind of spoiled . . . she played with her dolls even [when] she become a young lady."

In her recent studies on Nelson Island which examine the symbolic dimensions of Eskimo culture, Ann Fienup-Riordan notes that a girl's first menstruation is referred to as "the putting away of the dolls." Commenting further, Riordan writes:

These miniature dolls provide a condensed image of the Qaluyaarmiut attitude towards the procreative process. They are constructed from wood or ivory and often made with a hole running from the head to the base of the body, as through their use and their constant recycling the process of human regeneration was accomplished. Young girls were forbidden from using dolls during the winter or inside the house. Their use was restricted to the outside, and the summer season, marked by the return of the birds. Their dormancy in the interior of the house (nepiaq or enae, whence neliaq [womb, lit. made house]) during the winter, and their emergence in the summer as the playthings of immature girls replicates both the transformation of their owners through puberty restrictions into women capable of giving birth and the birth process itself. It seems only appropriate that a girl would be required to put away her irianiaguaq *(lit. pretend child) between the time she could play with it and the time when she could produce her own.*

(Fienup-Riordan:in press, 1982)

Joe Friday, a Chevak elder who remembers carving dolls for his own children, talked at length about *cugat*,

Fig. 8. *Joe Friday, Chevak elder and village historian, used to carve dolls for his daughters, and he spoke with us at length about the custom of playing with dolls.*

or play dolls (fig. 8). "In those days, the people used to make dolls of the family pairs, of their moms and dads. At this time, like at this time of the season, springtime, the people, and especially children, would start making dolls to play with.

"The kids—girls used to make dolls like in—so many dolls so that they'd be like family. Each doll—when it's time to eat, they'd let 'em eat, and when it's time to go to bed they'd pretend to let 'em go to bed. Time to wake up, they'd let 'em wake up too, as well, and that's the way they used to make them dolls. They used to treat 'em like a real live family group.

"They would pretend to have a doll— they would pretend to have a dad go out seal hunting or check the fish trap. They would pretend to let him go out and come back and they'd have another doll who would be like his son or daughter to go out and meet him—person like, just like real life.

"They pretend to make these people living like human beings like us. They would let them do things that people— real people do. Whenever they, one of the dolls, a female doll wants to make clothing, they would take both hands and let them make something. And when it comes to a man, for carving, he would take both hands, both arms, and let him do some carving, pretend that he's carving just like a real man would . . . .

"They would play with these dolls from springtime all the way through summer time, and then they would put them away at the beginning of winter to prevent them from bad weathers.

"They were told not to mess around with those dolls that they had, not to mess around or put them any old place whenever they were done with them. They said they were treated like real things, real live things . . .

"There was a village one time that—when they were playing with dolls during the wintertime, the season came about to be spring, and this certain village was still winter, and all those birds—ducks—were walking on top of the snow, and they didn't realize that the place around them was summertime, but the village inside was winter."

Friday said that the dolls were made mostly out of cloth, but that they also had dolls with wood faces and ivory faces: "The ones with the wooden face—their faces were carved like a real face, but ivory ones were just—they're pretty much eyes and nose."

E.W. Nelson reported seeing similar doll families, complete with toy boots, miniature grass mats, and mouse skin bedding, on Sledge Island near Nome in 1890's (1899:345). Cloth rag dolls and carved wood and ivory dolls with accompanying miniature households, Siberian type baby dolls, improvised walrus lower jawbone dolls, occasional "paperdoll" cutouts usually made of bark, jointed, movable dolls, and the simple ground squirrel clad figures made presently in Kivalina seem to span the range of dolls made as playthings for Eskimo children.

Dolls Made For Sale

There are, however, many other types of Eskimo dolls, most of which have been made for sale to the tourists or collectors' market since the late nineteenth century. (Some dolls made for ceremonial purposes were probably made until fairly recent times as well.) Dolls made for sale are essentially craft or fine art objects, and they fall into several distinctive regional types, as do the toy dolls. The nine basic regional doll types we have identified include the following: reindeer horn dolls with removable parkas, which are confined exclusively to

Shishmaref and Brevig Mission; whalebone dolls carved in Shishmaref; portrait style dolls with very realistic carved wood faces and meticulously detailed clothing from the Kotzebue area or from women who originated from there, (it can be seen in the closeup of Dolly Spencer's traditional lady doll that some of these portrait dolls are almost rendered lifelike); ivory-faced dolls, often depicting a mother packing a child, which are made primarily in Wales, some in Teller, and possibly in Little Diomede (these have mask-like faces); realistic ivory-headed dolls with heads carved in full round, often with

detailed features and with carved ivory hands from the village of Savoonga on St. Lawrence Island; activity dolls, or doll "models", which are made by several women over a wide area, although they are more prevalent in Southwest Alaska; and coiled grass basketry dolls, made by a few women in Southwest Alaska, (although they seem to have antecedents in the archaelogical record of other areas [Ford:1959:224]).

Leather or skin faced dolls are found everywhere, with commercially tanned skin faces appearing to be more common in Southwest Alaska, and "home-

Rob Stapleton

Fig. 9. *Grass for basket making hangs on the side of a shed in Kongiganak, drying and curing.*

testine, can be tanned only at certain seasons. Clement Ungott of Gambell describes the process: "(The) white material there, we men go out hunting and brought in whole length of bearded seal . . . Then she cleaned the inner part and put the inside out; then she have to scrape the inside part too." Clement goes on to say that the skin must be cleaned and rinsed many times per day for several days, changing the water often. "Then she take it outside and inflate it, blow it out . . . and as soon as it's blown fully inflated, she had to put it out to air dry. The wind blows, and the cold air blows it dry — white like that."

Another widely used, seasonally collected material is the pelt of the Arctic ground squirrel, which must be trapped in the springtime. Molly and Vincent Tocktoo of Shishmaref use steel traps which they set up "when the squirrels first come out from the ground, through the snow in the slope or in the hills, and that way it's easier." Vincent's grandparents used baleen snares for trapping squirrels, but he has never used one. Herbert Anungazuk of Wales told us that during the breeding season, squirrel skins are "peppered with wounds," and he recommends trapping them in early spring or late fall.

Mary Azean (interpreter for Mary Black in Kongiganak) describes the seasonal process used in preparing beach grass for basket or dollmaking: "It's really hard to get the good ones to make baskets out of, and it's only in fall time that we get them, while they're green, or when

Fig. 10. Dolly Spencer unrolls a length of oogruk (bearded seal) intestine, which was used in sewing waterproof garments and is still used in making traditional rain gear for dolls.

tanned" winter-bleached seal skin or caribou faces common further north. Within this category of leather-faced dolls fall the idiosyncratic dolls with expressive, often funny, and even ugly, features, which seem to comprise a tradition local to Chevak.

The ninth category consists of wood faced dolls that differ dramatically from the Kotzebue portrait style. Wood-faced dolls, like those of skin, can be found in every region, but it is those from many Southwest Alaskan villages, especially Eek, which are easiest to recognize. These are the dolls which appear to claim Okvik lineage. They have oval or heart shaped faces with slender noses in

a distinctive nose-brow ridge arrangement. Each of these regional types will be dealt with more thoroughly in the section on individual dollmakers and their work.

Tools and Materials

Many of the women included in the exhibit clothe dolls with skins or furs which come from animals also acquired for food, especially seal and caribou. The tanning processes for certain types of skin, such as winter-bleached seal skin are similar in many regions, and all the tanning procedures are very time consuming. Some, like the white skin or in-

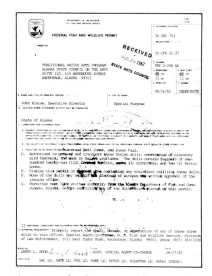

Fig. 11. Federal permit authorizing the State Arts Council to have dolls in the exhibit which have bird feather parkas.

Fig. 12. *A family's drying rack with several caribou skins in Anaktuvuk Pass.*

shading off their color from green to white . . . There's lots of work on the grasses . . . we pick the ones that we know will be the best to sew with, and then we come home from getting them. We braid them and hang them where they will dry really good (fig. 9) and put them away—in paper bags and plastic bags. Let them stay there for awhile and then after that, if we're going to use them, we dampen them and then start.''

Urban dollmakers like Dolly Spencer and Eva Heffle value traditional materials highly, often traveling or writing to home villages to get skins for sewing. Dolly Spencer describes one such trip: ''One time I told my sister, Mary, I need some oogruk gut, so I went home in the springtime . . . she froze me an oogruk gut, so I been hauling my frozen oogruk gut in my suitcase and come home and cure it myself (laughter). Sometimes they load me down with oogruk.'' Dolly also writes relatives and friends in several villages regularly, offering to pay for materials that other sewers may not use, such as wolverine head and tail fur, which she uses for hair and trimmings for her dolls

(fig. 10). All of the dollmakers buy materials at times and often at considerable expense. Eva Heffle noted that untanned seal skins now cost as much as eighty dollars each.

Some materials traditionally used by dollmakers are now subject to government restrictions. Historically, bird-feather parkas made from such species as loon, cormorant, eider duck, puffin, and murre were worn in many areas, and they were often depicted in miniature on dolls. Laws prohibiting the sale of migratory bird feathers were originally enacted in 1918, and supplemented in 1972. For many years, isolated skinsewers did not know such laws existed and continued to produce feather-clothed dolls, although few still do. The Arctic loon skin hunter doll by Mary Nash of Chevak, as well as Josephine Ungott's dolls dressed in cormorant and auklet feathers, were made possible through the use of the special permits issued to the Alaska State Council on the Arts by the U.S. Fish and Wildlife Service (fig. 11).

Other restricted materials which cause problems for dollmakers are seal and

caribou hides. Non-Natives are forbidden to hunt seals, so dollmaker Dolly Spencer, who now lives in Homer, must hunt without the help of her husband, and she says with a laugh that the seals have little to fear: ''I go seal hunting, but I'm a poor shot anymore.'' [Interviewer: ''I didn't know women went seal hunting.''] ''Yeah. I have to. They tried to stop me from seal hunting, my sister and I. There seem to be very few Natives here, so I wrote to . . . Senator Stevens. I wanted to seal hunt, otherwise I have to freight my seal oil down here, and there's quite a few widows here, so whenever I get a seal I share seal oil with them, or else they would be sending for some up north. They try to get us so we seal hunt way out in open water, way out there—said I can go out with my little boat. Sometimes the weather gets really nasty . . . they think I slaughter seals. I don't hit'em (laughter) . . . my husband can run the boat but not shoot . . . . Last year I didn't even get one . . . . The seal oil—last year my sister sent me a can of seal oil down here. It cost me sixty bucks.''

Susie Paneak of Anaktuvuk Pass says that restrictions on caribou hunting in

Fig. 13. *Maggie Komonaseak, Wales, shows the patterns she uses in dollmaking.*

the area have caused a shortage not only of doll and mask making materials, but of skins for villagers' clothing and necessary food (fig. 12). Her son George says that at times when the season is open on caribou, the hides are unsuitable for clothing. The animals are rutting and the "hair is too big." Susie puts it more bluntly, saying that if there was "no Fish and Game . . . lotta clothes."

Reindeer and caribou fawn skins, used primarily in the north, are another scarce material needed by several dollmakers. Margaret Ahlalook of Wainwright, who is a widow, often has to buy caribou fawn skins, even though half-wild caribou come as close as the village airstrip. And when she does buy skins, some parts are not suitable for dolls or clothing: "there's a lot of dead skin. The belly's no good, legs are not good." Newborn reindeer fawns are often found dead near Shishmaref, so when one is found, Molly and Vincent Tocktoo "don't buy it, they just rescue it" to use for doll clothing. Now that existing herds are under individual ownership and fawn skins are hard to obtain, there is an increased use of ground squirrel skins for doll clothes. The reindeer herd of St. Lawrence Island is now almost completely wild making fawn skins a rare material there as well.

A brick-red or ochre colored trim is often used on Eskimo garments, masks, wood carvings, and dolls. The use of this color is extremely widespread, from the Lapps to the Western Eskimo (Hatt:1969:16).

This favored red color is obtained from alder bark in an involved lengthy process. Annie Alowa says the she finds alder for dyeing as "driftwoods, like pieces of vines or something drifted in." She puts the bark and water inside a seal poke, ties the arms, and says the next step is to "sew it up the skin sides, but use the armhole to put all the willow dyes inside. Tie the armhole and rub them . . . when we soak the willow dyes that water becomes real red." Skinsewers commonly refer to the plant used for red dye both as willow and alder, although it is technically alder. Apparently any of the various kinds of alder can be used to make red dye, although Dolly Spencer, when she first began to make dolls and mukluks, once tried to make willow dye while she was living in Glennallen: "I don't know how to select my willows . . . I got my stepdaughter and my daughter . . . so I go out and cut a willow and they scraped and scraped . . . I dried it real

Fig. 14. *Maggie Komonaseak, Wales, uses an ulu to cut a piece of seal skin for doll clothing.*

good in the oven, and then I just said, now I'm going to dye some skins so I can make you girls some more mukluks.' It's about 56° below up there. It didn't get red. I got the wrong willow."

St. Lawrence Island sewers, as well as carvers and skinsewers from several other regions, often use a crumbly reddish-orange iron oxide which they refer to as red ochre or cinnabar. (Nordenskiold identified it as limonite in *Voyage of the Vega* (1882:323)). This red dye is spread directly on skins with hands or a brush.

Dorothy Jean Ray writes that "red color, especially from minerals, appears to have had a magical meaning for all Arctic people" (1981:19), and says that chunks of red minerals were sometimes presented as gifts and used as amulets.

Josephine Ungott of Gambell mentioned one "very old method" of obtaining red coloring: "They used to dye them with blood of a long time ago," hitting themselves on the nose to obtain the blood. Oswalt refers to the same process in *Alaskan Eskimos*, stating that the blood was obtained by "puncturing the inner surface of a nostril with a sharp stick. The blood might be mixed with urine and was applied with a squirrel-hair brush" (1967:157).

Several of the dollmakers use patterns. Maggie Komonaseak of Wales cuts her patterns out of plastic lids so that they will store easily and last longer (fig. 13). Others make patterns from cardboard. Almost without exception, the women use ulus (fig. 14). An ulu is the traditional semi-circular Eskimo woman's knife used for cutting skins and thread. (Ulus are also used to cut meat and fish.) Ethnographer Dinah Larsen underlines the importance of the ulu, commenting that it "is unlikely ever to be supplanted in the village by a mass produced product. Every woman owns one and often several of varying sizes" (1972:40). Thread used is most often dental floss or waxed thread, although for some women sinew is a first choice. Dolly Spencer does all her sewing with sinew when making dolls. Caribou-back sinew is hard to obtain in many areas nowadays, and many women must make do with substitutes. Interestingly, Caroline Penayah of Copper Center is currently using whale sinew obtained from relatives on St. Lawrence Island. At least two dollmakers, Amelia Kingeekuk and Josephine Ungott, both of St. Lawrence Island, still crimp tiny doll mukluk soles (as well as full-size soles) with their

Fig. 15. *Eek, a southwestern Alaska village, May 1982.*

Rob Stapleton

teeth. Other dollmakers use pliers or an ulu or knife blade. Both commercial metal and handmade bearded seal thimbles are used for sewing. Many tools, such as skin scrapers, are often handed down through generations of sewers. Male artists like Vincent Tocktoo and Elliot Olanna, both from Shishmaref, use traditional carving tools, such as the mattock, a chisel-like tool of ancient origin described by Nordenskiold in *The Voyage of the Vega* (1882:313).

Stuffing used in dolls ranges from dried beach grass and clipped reindeer hair to the synthetic stuffing from Margaret Ahlalook's plaid couch. Margaret's daughter, Martina Panik, says with laughter, "when she first got it [the couch], it was really fluffy. I didn't know she got it [the doll's stuffing] from there."

Marketing Techniques

I have already mentioned that most of the dollmakers use proceeds from doll sales as a substantial supplement to family income, while a few support

themselves almost entirely from earnings based on sewing.

When objects once made for use, such as play dolls, began to be made for sale, "those Eskimos whose lives were altered by a changing economy . . . fell back on activities they knew best, hunting and carving," and it can be presumed that women began sewing for sale as well. "Unfortunately, their originality and inventiveness were often curbed from the start by the narrow demands of the traders" (Ray:1967:82). On St. Lawrence Island, an influx of military personnel in the late 1940's was a great boom to sales of skin clothing, as well as wall hangings, dolls, and toys (Hughes:1960:197). Dinah Larsen, in a 1972 report, discusses the souvenir market for such items as dolls, masks, and ivory carvings, saying that in Northwest Alaska at least, the market could be expected to expand because of increased tourism. However, Larsen also states that "production of objects of this type does not appeal to many persons," so that souvenir production may "remain limited to a cottage-type industry, practiced by a few talented individuals" (1972:40). This prediction, at least for dollmakers, seems to have been correct.

One of the several BIA reports on Alaskan Native art production notes that "as better paying employment opportunities are opened to Native groups, it should be expected that they will leave their traditional handicraft way of life and enter the specialized wage and salary economy," referring to this as a "desired transition" (1964:11). This report identifies dolls as a handicraft product, saying that "the markets in which these dolls find their way will be those in which the buyers are collectors." Three women of Nikolski are cited in the 1964 report as dollmakers. The most productive of the three was able to make one doll per day which she could sell for five dollars. When the cost of skins, beads, needles, and other materials was itemized, the average cost of producing such a doll came to four dollars, *not* including direct labor.

Alaska Native Arts and Crafts (ANAC), for years the primary marketing outlet for Native arts in the state, was unofficially established in 1937 and remains a major outlet to this date. An ANAC catalog from the fifties cites at least three types of available Eskimo dolls, including reindeer horn dolls, and indicates that they were abundant and were available in many sizes. Other current outlets for dolls include the gift shop at the Native hospital in Anchorage, galleries and dealers all over the state, and direct sales to tourists and collectors. Caroline Penayah of Copper Center takes many of her dolls to the Native hospital gift shop on consignment ''just like everybody else.'' Dollmakers span the range, from those who only make dolls of museum quality to those who produce for a tourist market. Caroline Penayah has both a production line doll and a museum quality doll. She deliberately makes several kinds of dolls, refering to one as a ''money-making'' doll. The other three types are ''museum'' dolls like the one Penayah made for this exhibit.

Many dollmakers get mail orders constantly from people they don't even know. Such pressure from private orders was a factor in Caroline Panayah's move out of Anchorage: ''Too much involved for work; lots of customers and after awhile they get old and I just couldn't stand it anymore.'' Floyd and Amelia Kingeekuk of Savoonga also have more orders for dolls than they can fill, as do many other dollmakers. Most complete dolls when they need money or have extra time available. Although orders are welcome and are a source of income, they may conflict with seasonal subsistence activity and so be a mixed blessing at times.

Pricing varies greatly, increasing as inflation affects villagers, as well as when certain doll types become extremely popular. The early work of most dollmakers included in the exhibit was priced very modestly. Reindeer horn and ivory dolls made in Shishmaref during the 1930's sold for as little as two dollars each, while Susie Brown of Eek sold many dolls for $3.50 a piece during the 1940's. Eva Heffle was elated when she sold her first doll for ten dollars, and Martina Oscar, who makes activity figures, sold her first dolls for twelve dollars each. Fortunately for dollmakers, times have changed. The prices for dolls in this exhibit range from seventy-five dollars to fifteen hundred dollars.

Dollmakers and Their Regions

Effort was made to represent each cultural and linguistic region somewhat equally, highlighting well known dollmakers from each area and attempting to represent the very broad spectrum of materials used in dollmaking as well.

Some villages and regions, such as Chevak, Eek and the Nome area, abound in talented dollmakers, making choice complicated. Other areas have fewer women making dolls.

Southwest Alaska (Yup'ik)

Southwest Alaska encompasses a vast area stretching from Bristol Bay to Norton Sound, inland and along the coast of the Bering Sea, including Nelson and Nunivak Islands. The drainages of both the Yukon and Kuskokwim Rivers are in this region, which is inhabited by Yup'ik speaking Eskimos. The area is rich in natural resources, including waterfowl, abundant fish, and land mammals. Joe Friday, Chevak elder, describes the region in these terms in *Alaska Geographic*: ''We had absolutely nothing. We took care of ourselves with what nature had to offer. We made use of everything and did not want.'' (Vol. 6:No. 3:117). The Yukon-Kuskokwim delta is also the region with the most dollmakers, and from which the bulk of mythology about dolls and their manufacture was derived during the course of this project.

Of the eighteen dollmakers represented in the exhibit, seven are from Southwest Alaska. One of the most unusual dolls is the coiled grass basketry doll pair made by Mary Black of Kongiganak, on Kuskokwim Bay (fig. 15). Black's more conventional coiled baskets are citied by

Saradell Ard Frederick as: ''Three-dimensional examples of traditional art which exhibit superior technique plus occasional invention . . . fashioned of salt water grass and dyed seal gut'' (1972:37).

From the shore of Norton Sound to the Kuskokwim, women were credited with weaving grass mats, umiak sails, bags, baskets, and curtains (Mason:1970:395). Several dollmakers had much to say about the virtues of beach grass and its many uses. Helen H. Smith of Hooper Bay related a tale of how the use of grass saved her father's life: ''like if you fall in the water and if there's any grass around you could still use it under those wet clothes . . . One time my father fell in when he was hunting seal. It was month of January, and it's the coldest month, so he went up the hills. He gathered up all those [grasses] . . . then he hurry up, wring out his clothes, and put those grass next to his skin.'' Helen says that the grass kept her father warm and dry, but that his outer clothes were frozen so stiff that he was rendered nearly immobile by the time he reached home.

Both twined and coiled beach grass baskets are made, but the dolls in the exhibit are examples of the coiling technique, which involves an inner bunched grass coil foundation sewn continuously to adjoining coils with a whip stitch (fig. 16). Ray states: ''Each village has developed its own style of coiling tech-

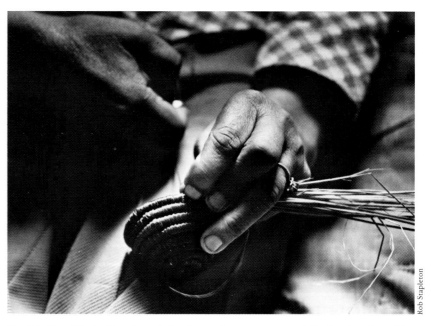

Fig. 16. *Mary Black, Kongiganak, begins work on a new grass doll, showing the coiling method used in grass doll making and grass basketry.*

niques, basketry shapes, and sometimes, designs'' (1981:63). She pinpoints the origin of grass basketry dolls at Hooper Bay in the mid-1970's, but also states that Ethel Montgomery, formerly with the ANAC store in Juneau, reported seeing two such dolls in 1949 (1981:130). At least one grass doll has been found in the archaeological record, discovered by James A. Ford at the late prehistoric Nunagiak site near Wainright (1959: 224). Pictured in Ray's book is a doll woven by Viva Wesley of Mekoryuk in 1978 (1981:130), and there must be at least half a dozen other practitioners of this relatively recent, unique art form in the delta region.

Mary Black, fifty-eight year old basket-maker who was born on Nelson Island, has been making coiled grass dolls for more than five years. Although she said she had imagined making such dolls — ''in her imagination she start sewing and imagine how that basket would be like a person'' — she did not make one until commissioned to do so. Basketry dolls are not an art form she particularly enjoys making, saying ''that she has a hard time making shape of the basket did . . . under the shoulder, starting to make the arms, and especially between the legs.'' Her dolls, not including the time it takes to pick, braid, and dry the necessary grasses, can take up to one month to finish. And the dyed seal gut she uses for decoration on both her baskets and dolls involves a lengthy preparation process in itself (fig. 17).

Chevak dolls comprise a very distinct tradition, also of fairly recent origin. The single most recognizable characteristic of most dolls from this village is a pinched and twisted leather face, sometimes grotesque, often whimsical (fig. 18). One Chevak dollmaker was heard several years ago to remark in recognition of this unusual aesthetic: ''It's very hard to make an ugly doll.'' Many Chevak dolls are depicted doing common local chores such as carrying firewood, gathering eggs, or bringing home game animals.

Rosalie Paniyak, forty-eight, is perhaps best known of the dollmakers from Chevak. Her dolls are present in the collection of the Anchorage Historical and Fine Arts Museum and have become popular with doll collectors for what Dorothy Jean Ray terms ''a rather macabre awkwardness'' (1981:129). Paniyak is characterized by those who know her as an amazing, highly motivated woman who helps support her large family through dollmaking and

Fig. 17. *While visiting in Kongiganak, we spotted coils of seal intestine hanging in a porch, and the lady who had cleaned and prepared them agreed to let us photograph them. This intestine will be cut into strips and dyed before being used to decorate baskets and grass dolls.*

Fig. 18. *Close-up of doll by Rosalie Paniyak, Chevak, showing the humorous faces that typify Chevak dolls.*

more recently, with a job helping village elders do various chores.

Rosalie Paniyak began making miniature dolls as a child for her own use; she started making dolls for sale sometime prior to 1970. Her daughter Ursula says she thinks Rosalie began to make dolls somewhat earlier than the 1970's ''because a lot of her friends were basket makers and she wanted to try something new.'' The dolls are immediately

recognizable as her own: sometimes eccentric, always imaginative.

Mary Nash, another Chevak dollmaker, submitted a seal hunter doll dressed for winter time in an Arctic loon skin parka. Loons are only one of several birds used in historic Eskimo clothing. Mary Nash dolls are enigmatic pieces which do not fit the usual Chevak mold. Hers generally have carved wood faces, which she herself carves with an ulu. Nash, who is now forty-seven, began making dolls around 1957, using proceeds of doll sales that first year to buy Christmas presents. She often makes dolls which illustrate a specific concept, such as her Poor Man dolls. She characterizes the hunter doll dressed in the loon skin parka as representing ''the person that can do very well on subsistence,'' and says that loon skins were used not only because they are a relatively durable feather, but because ''the feathers are nice designs.'' Loons are cited in many studies for being particularly ''important in the belief system of the Eskimo. Bird figures were sewn onto the shaman's coat and were considered good guardian spirts'' (Ackerman:1967:70). Nash tries to make all the clothing on her dolls very realistic, ''like you see people wear.'' She may take up to three days to finish a single doll.

Two dollmakers were chosen from the village of Eek, another center of doll manufacture. There are two types of dolls made in Eek: the old man and old lady dolls with wrinkled leather faces, and a doll with a very stylized wood face. According to village residents, the wood-faced dolls were first made in the mid-1940's by Stella Cleveland and Grace White. (These women are no longer living.) Other ladies of Eek learned from Stella Cleveland and Grace White, and many have now passed the art on to their daughters. There seems to be little variation in dolls from Eek, but the village style is instantly recognizable.

One exception is the work of Susie Brown, sixty-nine. She makes the classic wood-faced dolls, but she has varied the tradition slightly by creating families of dolls. A mother doll holding a small child, a father carrying a seal, and a young boy with a bat and ball are stitched together side by side to form the family. Susie Brown began making dolls in 1946, and her dolls were her only source of income for many years. Recently, she has been making fewer dolls, filling only occasional orders, because she is afraid that she will lose her Social Security benefits if she sells too many dolls. Otherwise, she would still like to make more dolls.

The wood heads of the dolls are of willow, carved by Susie herself. The seal skin for the dolls mukluks comes from seals which her husband catches in the winter and spring. The dolls' parkas are usually made of muskrat skins she has tanned herself, or from rabbit skins ordered by mail from Anchorage. Other skins used for trim, wolf, mink and calf, are purchased by mail order, acquired by trade from other women in the village, or, in the case of mink, prepared from animals her husband has trapped or shot.

The other style of doll from Eek, the old lady and old man dolls, were said to have originated five or six years ago. The first old lady doll was made by a woman named Grace White (not the same person as the Grace White mentioned earlier), who entered the doll in a Native art contest in Anchorage and won a cash prize for it. Now there are several ladies in the village who make old people dolls.

Lou C. Brown, thirty, whose old man and old lady doll are featured in this exhibit, learned to make this style of doll from her mother, Martha Carter. The wrinkled leather faces are made by working from the inside, making gathering stitches in a zigzag pattern across the forehead and in u-shaped patterns on the cheeks. Lou Brown uses many commercially tanned skins, including rabbit, beaver, raccoon, sheep and deer. She sews in her free time, and sends most of her dolls to shops in Bethel or Anchorage. She also makes the wood-faced dolls, often a mother holding a child. When asked if she could name other ladies in Eek who made dolls, Lou quickly wrote out a list of fifteen names, proof of Eek's reputation as a center of dollmaking.

Helen H. Smith of Hooper Bay has been making dolls for fifteen years and says she is "still learning a lot of things." She works as an alcoholism counselor in the region and takes her sewing with her whenever she travels to other villages for her job. Helen learned to sew at the age of eight by watching her mother. She took up dollmaking several years ago as a way of supporting her large family after the death of her husband. At first it took her three days to finish a single doll, but now, if she has a large order, she can finish several in a day, using a small-scale assembly line method: "do the boots first, parkas, faces . . . ."

In explaining how materials were cut to the right size for sewing, Helen talked about a traditional Eskimo system of measurements, using one's body, and especially the hand as a unit of measurement (fig. 19). Patterns were unnecessary. Helen Smith also talked about various materials which were traditionally used for clothing—making socks or boots liners from soft grass, parkas from bird skins, waterproof seam inserts of decorative winter-bleached muktuk (oogruk) stomach. Helen said she wished someone would write "how the old people used to live long ago. We don't— when we're out of clothes—we don't run to the store. People used to make their own clothing. Sometimes, people, I used to see them, are just worn out until they get new ones. And bird skins were the warmest ones . . . sea ducks are the stongest ones . . . my grandma used to pass us fresh (sea duck) skins before they got bitter taste and then she let us chew—just like for tanning. We spit out the oil, then she hang them, or sometimes if it gets a little too oily, she soak them in water, and those are the best, the warmest parkas that we ever have." Helen went on to talk about the fancy loon skin parkas and king eider parkas, and explained how a duck would have been skinned if its skin was to be used in parka making.

Fig. 19. *Helen H. Smith, Hooper Bay, demonstrates some of the traditional Eskimo methods of measurement, using hand or leg lengths rather than patterns.*

Helen Smith is a natural educator, who, along with her sisters Natalia Smith and Neva Rivers, harbors a wealth of knowledge about the traditional arts and customs of her people. She is proud of her work and takes great care in making dolls: "It's just a little person . . . Every little thing. It's got to be perfect so when I put on them, when I turn them over, everything will look the same." The four dolls she made for this exhibit represent two female dancers, one male dancer, and a male singer-drummer. The headdresses on the female dancers are just one sign of Helen Smith's attention to detail. Each headdress has several rows of stitching, arranged in three strips. Helen explained that this pattern of stitching on the doll's headdress is her own family's insignia (fig. 20). She explained that when she grew up, each family had its own sign, and that this was painted or carved on to tools and weapons and also sewn into clothing, identifying the user or wearer as a member of a certain family. Helen's older sister, Natalia, said, "they got their own marks. They don't write it. They don't sign their names. They don't write it on the paper, but they got their own mark . . . if they have an accident or disappear or something out in the seas—if they wash up, all by their things, we know who they are."

The headdresses worn by the female dancer dolls are traditionally worn by Yup'ik women for special dances and ceremonies, and each female dancer also has small dance fans which she holds while dancing. The male dancer doll has been placed in a kneeling position, again a tradition of Yup'ik dance in southwest Alaska (fig. 21). The scene of dancers by Helen Smith is what is often referred to as an *activity doll* or a *doll model*, when one or more dolls are posed in a traditional activity, often accompanied by miniature props.

Another Yup'ik dollmaker known for her activity dolls is Martina Oscar. Martina, who grew up in Newtok and Tununak, now resides in Bethel. She was born c.1926, and she began making dolls in 1953. When she first made dolls, she used her grandfather for a model, posing the dolls in activities and work she had watched him doing. Nowadays she makes activity dolls in every kind of traditional activity, from a man making a fish trap to a woman making baskets or picking berries. The dolls have wires in their arms and legs so that they can be positioned in different poses.

Fig. 21. *These dancers are from Stebbins, a Yup'ik village on Alaska's coast. Men dance from a kneeling position in front of the women. Both use dance fans.*

Some researchers have suggested that activity dolls or doll models, such as those made by Oscar, Smith and Heffle, may have their origins in similar scenes made during the 1890's or later. Alaska State Museum curator, Bette Hulbert, says that such scenes were requested by collectors as mementos, representing such activities as "corralling caribou or geese, seal hunting on the ice, or festival scenes" (1976:22). Two very elaborate dance scenes are pictured in Ray's *Aleut*

Fig. 20. *The rows of stitching on this doll's headdress are a family insignia. Such marks were used as family signatures on clothing, tools and weapons for Hooper Bay Eskimos.*

and Eskimo Art (1981:152-53). Some of these doll scenes were carved in wood, while others were carved of ivory (fig. 22).

However, there may be another origin for activity dolls, especially for the miniature ones such as Martina Oscar and other Bethel women make. These dolls may be an extension of the small dolls Martina herself played with as a child. These play dolls—some were rag dolls and some had ivory faces and cloth bodies—were made to do all kinds of daily activities and often had little beds and tools made for them. Little girls would have entire families of these miniature dolls, made for them by older relatives. The dolls which Martina makes today are not made for play, but it is possible that they have been developed from the older style, miniature toy dolls.

St. Lawrence Island (Siberian Yup'ik)

Today the Siberian Yup'ik people of St. Lawrence Island live in two villages: Gambell, situated on a natural gravel spit at the Northwest cape of the island, and Savoonga, on the north side near Kukulik Cape. St. Lawrence is the largest island in the Bering Sea, located

less than forty miles from the Siberian coastline, where the closest cultural relatives of the island's inhabitants lived until very recently. In "prewhite days the St. Lawrence Eskimo knew of the Alaskan mainland only indirectly" (Hughes:1962:4), so close were their Siberian ties. The art and traditions of those people can still be traced directly to their Siberian origins.

Some of the finest examples of primitive art in the world, the prehistoric Okvik ivory doll figurines of the Punuk Islands, came from this region, and contemporary artists from both Savoonga and Gambell produce ivory carvings and skinsewing which rival any in Alaska today. There are many dollmakers working currently on St. Lawrence, of whom Josephine Ungott (Gambell), Annie Alowa (Savoonga), and Floyd and Amelia Kingeekuk (also of Savoonga) are represented in this exhibit. Another dollmaker originally from Savoonga, Caroline Penayah, has moved away from the island and her work will be discussed in another section.

Josephine Ungott was born in Gambell and lives there now with her son Clement, his wife Irma, and four grandsons. She began making female dolls over fifty years ago when she was a young

63

girl, and started making male dolls in the early 1970's at a customer's request.

Examples of her work can be seen in many museum collections, and one female doll traveled widely with the 1977 exhibit ''Survival: Life and Art of the Alaskan Eskimo.'' She credits a relative, Flora Tungiyan, with the origins of the female doll dressed in a seal gut parka that she and several other Gambell dollmakers currently produce.

Josephine's male hunter doll is clothed in a bird skin parka made from the neck skins of five cormorants. A full size parka of this type might require as many as twenty-five cormorant skins, or the skins of thirty-five smaller birds such as murres. Bird skin parkas were once prized as warm, extremely waterproof garments. Josephine herself wore one as a young girl, although ''she didn't like to wear it [because] they were real easy to tear,'' and she was an active child. Her son, Clement, says a bird feather parka is ''very light and it's very warm. You can stand the weather.'' Clement wishes that he owned one now.

Historically, bird feather parkas were made widely over coastal Alaska and other Arctic regions by both Eskimos and Aleuts from many species of birds. Dorothy Jean Ray, quoting Veniaminov, says that in the early nineteenth century little Aleut children ''wore garments made from 'eagle skin with down,''' and that eagle skin garments were found in Prince William Sound as well (Ray:1981:53). According to Stefansson, a swan skin ''plucked of all but the finest down makes good clothes for children'' (1919:215). Loon skin socks were in use as recently as 1970-71 in Nunapitchuk (Oswalt:1972:86), and Clement Ungott believes that at least one Gambell elder has, and occasionally still uses, a bird feather parka.

The hunter by Josephine Ungott carries a pack and rifle case of winter-bleached seal skin. Clement says, ''this is the pack we carry when we're hunting. It's a pouch that we carry. It contains our hunting gear like seal hooks, retrieving hooks, some strings, ropes that we use to tie seals when you get seals . . . Our ammunition is in there. Our knives are in there. Emergency packs, first aid and stuff like that we pack nowadays.'' Clement's own pack and rifle case, both made of shaved young bearded seal (a dark grey brown leather) by Josephine, are waterproof and highly efficient. The

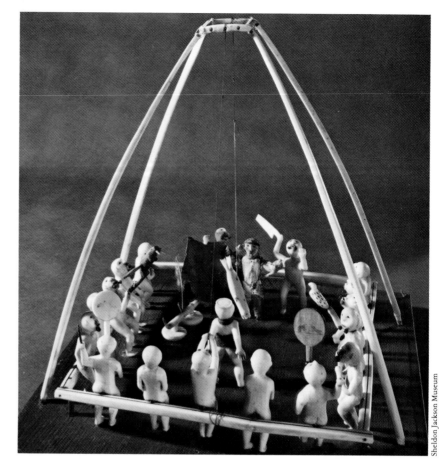

Sheldon Jackson Museum

Fig. 22. *This activity scene of ivory figures, now part of the Sheldon Jackson Museum collection, was collected from the Kuskokwim River area in the 1890's. Such scenes, often made at the request of collectors, may be the prototype of today's activity dolls.*

fur inside the gun case is said by Clement to protect his rifle from rusting.

The female doll made by Josephine Ungott is wearing a festive opaque air-dried seal gut parka decorated with the maxillae and topknots of 122 crested auklets saved from auklets acquired for food over the past several years. Unlike the intestine parka worn by Rosalie Paniyak's ''Mud-house'' doll, which is an everyday raincoat, this parka is meant for special occasions such as dressing up, dancing, or visiting.

Remnants of gut parkas have been found in the prehistoric archaeological record of several areas, continuing the use through historic and contemporary times, with widespread distribution among Eskimo and Aleuts. Bearded seal intestine is the most widely used material, but whale bladder, and the skin of ''a great whale's tongue'' were used at times by the Koniag Eskimos (Oswalt:1979:242). Some raincoats were sewn with grass, seal whiskers, or fine

feathers from certain waterbirds for waterproofing of the seams according to John Bockstoce, who quotes both Nelson and Murdoch (Bockstoce:1977:93). Gut strips comprising the parka body were sewn vertically or horizontally, varying with the region of origin. Nordenskiold noted the widespread use of gut skin garments, saying that on St. Lawrence it appeared ''that gut clothes are made for sale to other tribes; otherwise it would be difficult to explain how Kotzebue's sailors could in half an hour purchase at a single encampment 200 coats of this kind'' (1832:350). Gut parkas must have had some special significance, for Johan Jacobsen saw sixty of them distributed as gifts in the kashim during a single night at Ikniktok (1977:136), and Lantis says that they were worn ''as a symbol of spring hunting'' (1947:55). Ray cites the gut parka as ''often the principal garment worn by the *angakok* [medicine man] when calling forth his spiritual helpers'' (1959:13).

Sea mammal intestine had many other uses, including sewing bags and house windows. Dolly Spencer recalls such windows: "Walrus gut, seem like they are salted down pretty much as it's white; not as transparent as this [oogruk gut]. This is what we used for our windows in our sod houses when I was growing up . . . sew it together and use it for [windows] . . . transparent."

Floyd and Amelia Kingeekuk, from the village of Savoonga, also dressed their hunter doll in a gut parka (this one is walrus gut), calling it a "formal type of parka for when you want to dress up." Floyd says this style is worn with a belt: "it inflates too; put air in it and they get . . . nicer looking." Parkas of this type also served as cold weather gear, and the Kingeekuks noted that the opaque white parka on their doll is a "windproof," not a rain parka.

The carved ivory face of the Kingeekuk doll is lifelike and elegant, so meticulous that is has an almost Oriental appearance. Amelia began making dolls nearly ten years ago, but the dolls with ivory faces are a collaborative effort and of fairly recent invention. Floyd is well known for his ivory carvings which are represented in the Anchorage Historical and Fine Arts Museum and Carrie McLain Memorial Museum in Nome, as well as many private collections, and it is he who carves the hands and faces for the dolls. He spends a great deal of time observing animals "to learn more how they're sitting on the ice," using the observations in his carvings. He used his own hands as a model for the Kingeekuk doll. His imagination seems boundless, and his plans for future dolls include a blanket toss scene with a moveable central figure and a doll with eyelids that blink. Amelia is equally talented and energetic. She is a member of the Savoonga Comedy Players, a traveling troupe of Savoonga women who base their skits on traditional St. Lawrence mythology and customs.

The Kingeekuk hunter doll wears a hairstyle once common to Eskimo men, the tonsure (fig. 23). Nelson writes that this style was "universally practiced by the Eskimo . . . whether on the American or Siberian coast" (1899:57). Naomi Giffen attributes Asiatic Russian origins to the hairstyle and says that variations on the length of the remaining fringe of hair were many (1930:51-52). When he was a young boy, Floyd Kingeekuk remembers seeing

Fig. 23. *Close-up of ivory-headed doll by Amelia and Floyd Kingeekuk, Savoonga. This male doll has a hair style traditional among Eskimo men several generations ago.*

one or two Gambell residents wearing the old-time hairstyle.

Fifty-seven-year-old Annie Alowa of Savoonga is the other dollmaker featured from this region. She is an enthusiastic woman who is a natural educator, taking great pride in the traditions of her people. She was village health aide for twenty-two years, and describes herself as "always busy, busy, busy" crabbing, trapping, fishing, carving, or sewing. The oldest in a family of thirteen children, Annie was taught by her father to carve when she was an adolescent, and she has been producing artwork of various kinds ever since. (She has been making dolls less than ten years.)

Annie Alowa's "favorite daughter" doll wears a hairstyle common to many generations of Siberian Yup'ik women (fig. 24), said by Annie to have been worn especially by a family's favored daughter. The beads braided into the hair are generally red, white and blue. They were once prized trade beads from Siberia. Oswalt says that beads ranked second to tobacco in popularity as a trade item among Eskimos (1972:75), and it is said that "literally tons of glass (trade) beads have been distributed in America" (Jenkins:1972:38).

The favorite daughter doll is accompanied by several traditional implements of a Siberian Yup'ik household, including a carved wooden platter, a seal gut sewing kit or accessory bag, a miniature seal skin scraper and a tiny

ulu. Large driftwood platters, sometimes with steamed rims and baleen stitching, were once used as communal food trays in Eskimo homes. Annie remembers the platters in her ancestral home at Gambell: "Big families have real long (ones), because in our great grandparents' house there was two families that stays in one big house . . . We used to have longer than this one (a four-foot platter)." Sewing kits and boxes are stilled used by Eskimo women, and each woman currently making such kits seems to have her own identifiable style. Early forms of these kits included carved and incised ivory needlecases and "housewives," skin bags which could be used rolled up and fastened for easy storage (fig. 25).

Another interesting feature of the Alowa doll are the tattoos engraved on her ivory face and hands (fig. 26). At least fifteen older St. Lawrence women (including Josephine Ungott and Flora Imergan) have such tattoos (fig. 27), and a few younger Siberian Yup'ik women are contemplating going through the traditional procedure. The designs which are extremely varied, are executed with water, needle, seal oil, and soot at puberty by an expert older woman or female relative. Josephine says that tattooing was designed "to be feminine,"

Fig. 24. *Caroline Penayah is wearing the traditional braids and hair beads worn by women on St. Lawrence Island for special occasions.*

Fig. 25. *Mary Pingayak, a Chevak dollmaker, examines her sewing tools and materials, including a "housewife," the striped fabric sewing kit used by many Eskimo women.*

and Annie Alowa states that favorite daughters often had designs all the way up their arms: "the favorite daughters always had those tattoos on so they could be hanged up like favorite things." Men also had tattoos, sometimes more specifically symbolic. Clement Ungott says that men were tattooed in various places (generally on limb joints) after killing their first polar bear, and Annie Alowa states that the sister of a "good runner, good wrestler, good man" had a

Fig. 26. *This doll by Annie Alowa, Savoonga, has been "tattooed" in the style of St. Lawrence Island women. There are still a number of older women who have tattoos, but the practice has been discontinued.*

Fig. 27. *Josephine Ungott, Gambell, is marking a fur for cutting. Her face and hands are tattooed in the traditional manner.*

tiny male figure tattooed on her forehead. Whaling captains were also apparently tattooed with their successes, as were people cured for various ailments or protected from unlucky circumstances by a shaman (Anderson & Eels: 1935:61,175).

Northwest Alaska and The Arctic Slope (Inupiat)

This region encompasses coastal Alaska from the vicinity of the Unalakleet River

north and east to beyond the Canadian border, including all of the Seward Peninsula, King, Diomede, Sledge (now unpopulated), and Barter Islands, as well as some inland communities such as Anaktuvuk Pass. This is the home of the Northern Eskimo, all Inupiaq speakers, who comprise roughly one-third of Alaska's Eskimo population. It is a vast and beautiful region, encompassing about one-fourth of the state, ranging from the maritime climate of parts of the Bering Sea coast to the rugged Brooks Range and tundra of the Arctic slope.

Dollmakers featured from northwest Alaska include Elliot Olanna, Molly and Vincent Tocktoo (all from Shishmaref), and Maggie Komonaseak of Wales. Dolly Spencer and Eva Heffle are both originally from the Kotzebue area but have moved away permanently from the village and their work will be discussed in a later section.

Shishmaref is an industrious village of about two hundred people situated on Sarichef Island on the northern Seward Peninsula. Reindeer herding, ivory and whalebone carving, and dollmaking all provide income for the residents of the village (fig. 28).

The doll type best known from this village is the reindeer horn doll with removable parka, said by Jack Herman Ningealook, a village elder, to have been invented by Andrew Tocktoo, Vincent Tocktoo's uncle, in the mid-1920's, at about the same time the Ningealook family started making dolls of the same type. Currently, at least fifteen horn dollmakers live in Shishmaref, and one or two live in Brevig Mission. Half of these dollmakers are husband and wife, sister and brother teams, with the man carving the body while the woman clothes it. The other dollmakers consist primarily of single or widowed women.

Steps in making the body of reindeer horn or large whalebone figure are as follows: First, the doll body must be roughed out with a chisel or Eskimo mattock. The mattock is the same instrument used in making such objects as wooden meat platters and is often a beloved instrument handed down through generations of male carvers. Then a series of files are used, ranging from very rough initially, to a finer one for finishing touches. A Dremel or "motor" tool is sometimes used at this stage if the bone is not too greasy. Sandpaper is used to finish the piece, and small handmade chisels (Elliot Olanna has six sizes) smooth the body and etch detailed work like face and arms. India ink is used for drawing in facial features.

Amos Kiyutelluk, fifty-two, who has worked at the Shishmaref Native Store for eleven years, says that in the mid-1960's, dolls were purchased by the store for three dollars each. Now the store pays twenty dollars per doll, buying more of them than ever in the past. Originally, horn dolls were carved with distinct male and female sexual organs (as were some prehistoric dolls), according to Jack Herman Ningealook, but this is no longer done. Ningealook says they ''tried to copy a man and female at first when they started making horn dolls, and then . . . buyers told them that they don't have to put them on because it's not good to put them on.'' Dorothy Jean Ray, referring to such detailed, anatomically correct carving practices, says: ''Animals, too, forfeited some of their former realistic features. For example, one of the carvers told me that the old Eskimo artists used to put a hole under the tail of a fox or wolf, but the missionaires told them it was wrong so they stopppped.'' (1961:15). Amos Kiyutelluk remembers when he was a young boy that a trader came every year by ''tugboat'' right after breakup, trading candy, clothing, and other merchandise for Native goods such as mukluks (Shishmaref women are still well known for being exceptional sewers), horn and ivory dolls, and reindeer products. Ningealook believes that these first doll buyers did not intend the dolls as toys but as souvenirs: ''the buyers wanted to buy a part of the Natives here, and that's the reason why they buy the dolls.''

Vincent and Molly Tocktoo, now in their mid-fifties, were commissioned to make Shishmaref reindeer horn dolls for the exhibit. Both Molly and Vincent were born in the village and have lived there all their lives (fig. 29). Vincent has been making horn and whalebone dolls since he was fourteen, learning the process from his father, Eddie Tocktoo. He uses no electric tools to make the bodies and says that if he is working fast he can rough out one horn doll in fifteen minutes. Molly is nearly as fast; she can make up three sets of doll clothing in one day. Vincent works at construction jobs in the summer, supplementing family income by making dolls and freight sleds, but when he is out of work, horn doll manufacture supplies most of the Tocktoo's income.

Molly and Vincent disagree on exactly who is the dollmaker. In an interview with the Tocktoos, interpreter Esau Weyiouanna comments: ''[Molly says] I think the person that carves the horn dolls is the boss, but Vincent says that it takes lots of work to make parka. I think they both make the horn doll . . . he say he can carve horn doll anytime, but it takes time to make parkas, and he say that she's the most important person in making the dolls because she makes the parkas and stuff.''

Finding reindeer horn for the doll bodies is becoming increasingly difficult because herds are now under private ownership. Horn must be bought in bulk, selling for as much as twenty-dollars per pound. Some horn doll bodies have a greenish color, indicating that the horn used is an old one found lying on the tundra. Molly says the her whole family looks out for reindeer horn when they are on camping trips: ''even when we go berry picking, whenever we see horns we pick them up and put them

Rob Stapleton

Fig. 28. *A home in Shishmaref, with a reindeer head in the foreground of the photo. Shishmaref is the center of reindeer horn doll making.*

Fig. 29. *Molly and Vincent Tocktoo, Shishmaref, relax at their kitchen table.*

in the boat and take them. Our grandsons learn now . . . that whenever they see horns laying around they take them back to their grandparents.'' Fawn skins are also scarce, so dolls now are frequently clothed in squirrel or seal skin garments.

Elliot and Emma Olanna also make reindeer horn dolls and stuffed dolls, but Elliott was commissioned to make

sculptural whalebone figures for the exhibit. Several men in Shishmaref are whalebone sculptors, carving objects which run in the gamut from small, fairly realistic doll forms to large abstract pieces. Melvin Olanna, well-known Shishmaref printmaker and sculptor, carved a full-size male adult hunter from whalebone in 1980. Interest in whalebone carving is stonger in this village than in any other, although

isolated whalebone carvers exist in Gambell and Wainwright, while bone mask makers can be found in Point Hope and Kivalina. Presumably, this interest in whalebone can be traced to workshops in 1981 in which Gabriel Gely, a Canadian arts specialist and artist who had worked in similar programs in Canada, came to Shishmaref to impart enthusiasm and new ideas to village carvers. Whalebone carving tapered off after Gely's departure, but has undergone revitalization in the last few years.

Elliot Olanna began carving at about nineteen, learning by watching his brother, Washington, and using his brother's tools. He stores his own tools in a beautiful traditional bentwood tool box handed down to him by his great-great-grandfather (fig. 30). Olanna refers to the doll family he made for the project as "play parents." This doll family style originated at the request of a trader in the late 1970's.

Whalebone is another material fast becoming scarce. Most whalebone is found on the beach, sometimes a long way from the village, and must be carried home by boat or stacked up for a return trip by the "owner". Elliot says, "[the whalebone] got to be old in order to be carved because when they are new they smell and they stick to your clothes." Scavenging for whalebone is an activity pursued now by many villagers. Those who do not carve, sell the material to artists who need it. A small percentage of "found" bone may be derived from coastal archeological sites, but most of it is picked up on the beach, unlike Canadian sculpture of a similar type which uses whalebone from old Thule culture house ruins (McCartney:1979:3).

Maggie Komonaseak, forty-six, of the coastal village of Wales, is the final northwest Alaskan dollmaker included in this section. She works jointly with her husband Silas, who carves the faces, and she says that she probably wouldn't make dolls without him. She works from patterns designed by her mother, Carrie Weyapuk. Maggie began making ivory-faced dolls in the late 1950's, following a village tradition of somewhat uncertain origin, although she says it may have been encouraged by a trader who placed higher value on ivory-faced dolls than those with skin faces. Ivory-faced dolls with flat, mask-like faces sewn to cloth head and body are made primarily in Wales, though a few come from Teller

Fig. 30. *A handmade bentwood tool box which has been passed down through several generations to Elliot Olanna.*

and occasionally from Little Diomede. Maggie Komonaseak makes up to fifty dolls a year, adding to family income while working full time as a cook at the school as well.

Many ivory-faced dolls, such as the one in the exhibit, are depicted packing babies. Packing babies is an idea so ingrained in Eskimo girls that Maggie remembers ''playing pack rocks,'' choosing oval shaped rocks and packing them inside parka or kuspuk as a young girl. Occasionally she substituted puppies for the role of ''baby.'' This method of carrying infants is an efficient one and is still practiced by women all over the Arctic (fig. 31). Ray has noted that a caribou tooth belt was sometimes used to secure a baby to its mother's back. Such a belt was reported to have curative powers; it was also a way of a woman's letting everyone know what a good hunter her husband was (1981:57).

Two dollmakers from the Arctic Slope region are featured in this exhibit: one from the coastal village of Wainwright and the other from Anaktuvuk Pass, in the heart of the Brooks Range. Seventy-three year old Margaret Ahlalook moved to Wainwright from a camp near Prudhoe Bay in 1934. She made her first doll at Barrow in 1943 at the request of a teacher, using the six dollars she earned to buy groceries, but most of her early dolls were sold to her grandfather, who had a little store. At one time she made two doll couples per week, but arthritis in her hands has slowed current production. She is proud of her meticulous stitching, and as her daughter Martina says, ''she always does her best to make things that would look good instead of just any old way.''

Anaktuvuk Pass, home of dollmaker Susie Paneak, sixty-seven, is situated in the center of one of three corridors penetrating the rugged Brooks Range. The village was permanently established around 1950. Prior to then, many present day Anaktuvuk villagers led a seminomadic life, ''roaming the land as they had for generations, traveling by dogteam and dwelling in caribou hide tents'' (Spearman:197:45). Susie Paneak, who was raised in this manner by her step-parents, Elijah and Mae Kakinya, says she misses those days.

Susie is apparently the only woman in Anaktuvuk who makes the caribou mask-faced doll, although it was her stepmother who probably originated a similar type about forty years ago. Susie

Fig. 31. *The Eskimo woman on the right is packing a baby in her parka. Dolls by Maggie Komanaseak and Margaret Ahlalook are mothers packing babies.*

Paneak's dolls are extensions of the typical Anaktuvuk style caribou skin face masks, which were invented as a Christmas joke by two village trappers in 1951. Simon Paneak, Susie's late husband, helped revitalize the mask idea in conjunction with several other men about five years after its original inven-

Fig. 32. *Caribou skin masks in the making in Susie Paneak's house in Anaktuvuk Pass.*

tion, and it has since become a distinctly regional art form (fig. 32). Masks provided the major source of income for the village until fairly recently, when scarcity of available caribou hides because of hunting restrictions and access to local construction jobs slowed mask making.

Susie sold her first doll for ten dollars and says that each doll takes nearly one month to make. She also makes a wide range of traditional caribou hide clothing when she has materials available, but she considers herself a mask maker primarily, not a dollmaker. Before she bagan working at a nearby construction camp as a part time bullcook, making masks was her only source of income.

Urban Dollmakers

Three dollmakers included in the exhibit are relocated, probably permanently, away from their home villages. Although their dolls nearly always reflect the traditional garments of home regions, their methods of obtaining materials, as well as many other aspects of their lives, are very different from rural Alaskan dollmakers.

Caroline Penayah, a fifty year old Siberian Yup'ik woman, was born in the village of Savoonga. She is a talented person with many personal dreams, some of which she fulfilled seven years ago by moving to a small farm near Copper Center: "I always thought about Chena River in Fairbanks, hot springs . . . I used to think about when I see those log cabins; those are my dreams. Some day one of these days I get out and garden, raising chickens and stuff like that. I thought about even [going] Outside in California." (fig. 33)

Caroline Penayah makes several kinds of dolls, differentiating between "money making" ones done fairly quickly for needed income, and those she considers museum quality. All of her dolls reflect Siberian Yup'ik tradition: "I really don't like to copy other people . . . when somebody asks me, like, would you do this like dolls from Bethel? I don't like that. I don't care how much I need the money." She continues to obtain materials needed for dollmaking from relatives on St. Lawrence Island and makes occasional visits to Savoonga, as well as buying some skins from furriers in Anchorage.

Caroline's female doll is wearing a *qallevak*, a traditional Siberian woman's coverall sometimes made of fawnskin, but often pieced of various black and white skins in a geometric or striped pattern. A full size *qallevak* made by Mrs. Lawrence Kulukhon in 1967, presently on display at the University of Alaska museum in Fairbanks, is made of pieced black and white ribbon seal strips. Ribbon seal is not rare, but its range is generally in the open sea, far from coastlines or villages in the north central Bering Sea, and is rarely hunted. The scarcity of its dramatic black and white pelt may have resulted in more common current use of mouton or pieced calfskin for the *qallevak*.

Eva Heffle, forty-six, Inupiat, of Fairbanks moved away from Kotzebue in 1959. She goes back to the village at least once every three years, visiting and obtaining materials for her dolls. She, like Caroline Penayah, is a woman with dreams. Someday she hopes to have her own shop in downtown Fairbanks, selling her own dolls and sewing, and she believes that an industrial sewing machine purchased recently with the assistance of the Institute of Alaska Native Arts (IANA) will help her achieve this goal. She is the only woman represented who has had a one woman show on her work. For this show, she was commissioned to create a complete set of

all twenty-seven activity doll models and several large scenes (fifty-four individual dolls in all.) This project was funded by a grant from IANA, culminating in a show early in 1982 at the University of Alaska Museum where the dolls are now permanently housed.

The activity scenes made by Eva Heffle include dolls such as the following: a woman chewing mukluk soles, an ivory carver, a woman making a birchbark basket, and a woman holding a baby, which was one of her first dolls, made in the early 1960's. She also makes four larger scenes, including the blanket toss exhibited here. One of the large scenes, which depicts an Inupiat family gathered around a fire in a gut tent, was inspired by eighty-nine year old "Arctic John" Etarook of Anaktuvuk Pass, a good friend of the Heffles.

Eva Heffle was raised by her grandmother, Mary Curtis, also a well known Kotzebue sewer: "I grew up with what Grandma put on the table." Eva was not interested in learning to sew until her early twenties, although she did take high school sewing classes from Lena Sours, her grandmother's sister. Dolly Spencer, also from Kotzebue, credits Lena Sours with the origins of commercial dollmaking in the village. Spencer says that in the late 1930's, Mabel Nielsen's husband carved a wooden doll head and took it to Lena Sours, who "fixed the body and made a doll. That was the first doll that was for sale." Spencer also says that Ethel Washington began making dolls at that time.

Eva Heffle's dollmaking began almost accidentally. While she was living in Seattle, she received a box from her mother containing two old doll heads, which she fashioned into dolls. She says the first doll had mukluks that "were *terrible* . . . I didn't know what I was doing, and I kept trying and trying." She says it took her years to learn, and it is clear that even today she is constantly experimenting with new ideas. Eva has painful rheumatoid arthritis and considers dollmaking "good therapy for hands and also they're just good pastime for me." She is optimistic about the arthritis, saying that if her hands ever weaken, "I've still got the ideas in my head . . . I can always teach." She is a woman of tremendous energy and courage: "I'm just not the type that sits around. I just like to do things."

The blanket toss scene made by Heffle for the exhibit represents an important

portion of the *Naluqutaq*, a festival held after the completion of a successful whaling season "which originally seemed to function as a propitiation of the spirit owners of the killed whales and a magical means for insuring good hunting for the following season" (Milan: 1964:41-42). The blanket itself is usually made up of several sections of bearded seal skin, and apparently everyone except very old people take turns jumping on it up to thirty feet in the air.

Dolly Spencer is Inupiat. She was born in Kotzebue in 1930 but lived primarily in the Cape Krusenstern area. Her mother taught her how to sew when she was about eight, and she also took sewing classes from Lena Sours at school in Kotzebue. She refers to Sours as "the oldest person of the original Kotzebue people." Kotzebue, a regional trading center, was a temporary place of residence for many people from surrounding villages during the summers, and it is only in recent decades that it has grown into a larger, more permanent settlement. Dolly Spencer's ancestors were from Ikpek, a coastal site which is now abandoned, between Wales and Shishmaref. (It is also Elliot Olanna's ancestral home and his family's summer camping place. Dolly is also distantly related to Molly Tocktoo, another Shishmaref dollmaker featured in this exhibit.)

The meticulously detailed birch faces of Dolly's dolls are nearly lifelike, often

Fig. 33. *Dollmaker Caroline Penayah feeds her chickens at her rural home in Copper Center, far removed from her birth place on St. Lawrence Island.*

carved as portraits of well known Alaskans like Jessie Carr, William Egan and Howard Rock, as well as Eskimo villagers in traditional garments (fig. 34). She has made a portrait doll of dollmaker Elliot Olanna, her old schoolmate, and once, upon request, even made a self-portrait doll. Dolly Spencer's dolls have become well known in Alaska, and she has won many ribbons and exhibit prizes for them.

Ethel Washington is sometimes credited as Dolly's mentor, but this apparently is not the case. Spencer did know the older dollmaker though, and occasionally watched her make dolls. Although she began sewing at an early age, Dolly did not begin making dolls until many years later when she lived in Glenallen. She sold her first doll, which had a blue jean body and dental floss stitching, for thirty dollars. Now her dolls sell for fifty times that amount and are painstakingly made of traditional materials, which she often travels far to get.

The use of all Native materials is important to Dolly. Her first dolls were of cloth and sewn with dental floss, but now she says, "when I start using skin, I says, well maybe people would rather have all skin materials—to be all Native. I use sinew and make it original. I try to make them look the way mother used to make them, the stitching and all . . . no matter if they're not fancy or fancy, I try to do it all how she would do it." All of Dolly's work is sewed with sinew which she has prepared herself from caribou tendons, stripping and twisting it into lengths for sewing. According to Dolly sewing with sinew is the only way to have truly waterproof seams, and although her dolls are not apt to encounter bad weather, this attention to realistic detail is important to her, even when making doll clothes.

The skins she needs for dollmaking can be difficult to get, living as she does now, on the Kenai Peninsula. She often writes to northern villagers to locate wolverine heads and tails, squirrel skins or oogruk gut. Getting skins tanned is another matter, and often a problem. Dolly has sent skins out to tanneries, but usually with unsatisfactory results. Squirrel skins are returned full of pock marks, and fox and otter pelts have been returned with the bellies missing.

Dolly Spencer is a very economical sewer. Nothing is wasted. In her house she has bags and bags of scraps of skins and furs, all being saved for use in the future sewing projects. When interviewed about her sewing, Dolly made diagrams to show how various animal skins are traditionally cut up for sewing so that there is no waste, and she commented more than once on the remarkable "fit" between the natural shapes of animal skins and man's clothing—how, for example, caribou legs, if tanned properly, are the perfect size and shape to make a pair of mukluks. As Dolly puts it: "I always say God sure knew what we were going to be shaped like when he made the animals."

When asked if she had played with dolls as a child, Dolly remarked that they had no play dolls then, that they sometimes played with puppies, pretending they were babies. She said of her mother's generation: "My mother's group was never into making play things. They were always sewing for survival, getting ahead in making new mukluks for each family. She never had time to mess with making us a doll." Perhaps it is ironic that nowadays, in Alaska, when making money—participating in a cash economy—becomes increasingly necessary, making dolls has, for many women, become a means of sewing for survival.

Most of the dollmakers chosen for this exhibit live in what many non-Natives would regard as harsh environment. Few of them have not been touched by the deaths of children or family members, by hunting or boating accidents, airplane crashes, or illness. Yet it is with skill and optimism that they continue to create the quality of work that can be seen in this exhibit. I am proud and honored that these people shared with us their lives, their talents, and at times, some of their pain. It is to the dollmakers and their families that this project is dedicated.

Fig. 34. *Dolly Spencer dolls. The one wearing a beret is Muktuk Marston, a famous Alaskan admired by Dolly.*

Works Cited in the Text

Ackerman, Robert E. 1967. Prehistoric Art of the Western Eskimo. *The Beaver* (Winnipeg) (Autumn):67-71.

Anderson, H. Dewey, and Walter Crosby Eells. 1935. *Alaska Natives: A Survey of Their Sociological and Educational Status*. Standford Unversity Press.

Atamian, Sarkis. 1966. The Anaktuvuk Mask and Cultural Innovation. *Science* 151, no. 3716:1337-1345.

Bockstoce, J.R. 1977. *Eskimos of Northwest Alaska in the Early Nineteenth Century*, Monograph Series No. 1, University of Oxford, Pitt Rivers Museum.

Carpenter, Edmund. 1973. *Eskimo Realities*. New York: Holt, Rinehart and Winston.

Collins, Henry B. 1973. Eskimo Art. *The Far North: 2000 Years of American Eskimo and Indian Art*, for the Anchorage Historical and Fine Arts Museum, 1-25. Washington: The National Gallery of Art.

Fienup-Riordan, Ann. 1982. *The Nelson Island Eskimo: Social Structure and Ritual Distribution*. Anchorage: Alaska Pacific University Press.

Ford, James A. 1959. *Eskimo Prehistory in the Vicinity of Point Barrow, Alaska*. American Museum of Natural History, anthropological papers, vol. 47, part 1.

Geist, Otto William, and Froelich G. Rainey. 1936. *Archaeological Excavations at Kukulik*. Miscellaneous publications of the University of Alaska, vol. 2.

Giffen, Naomi Musmaker. 1930. *The Roles of Men and Women in Eskimo Culture*. Chicago: The University of Chicago Press.

Gillham, Charles E. 1955. *Medicine Men of Hooper Bay*. New York: Mac-Millan Co.

Graburn, Nelson H. 1976. Introduction: Arts of the Fourth World. In: *Ethnic and Tourist Arts,* edited by Nelson H. Graburn, 1-32. Berkeley: University of California Press.

Hall, Edwin S., Jr. 1972. The Caribou Hunters of Anaktuvuk Pass. *Alaska Magazine* (November): 6, 7, 53-55.

Hatt, Gudmund. 1969. Arctic Skin Clothing in Eurasia and America: An Ethnographic Study. In *Arctic Anthropology*, translation by Kirsten Taylor, vol. 5, no. 2:3-132.

Hughes, Charles Campbell. 1962. *An Eskimo Village in the Modern World*. Ithaca: Cornell University Press.

Hulbert, Bette. 1976. *Alaska State Museum Bicentennial Catalog*. Juneau: Alaska State Museum.

Irving, Laurence. 1958. On the Naming of Birds by Eskimos. *Anthropological Press of the University of Alaska*, vol. 6, no. 2:61-77.

Jacobsen, Johan Adrian. 1977. *Alaskan Voyage 1881-1883: An Expedition to the Northwest Coast of America*, translation by Erna Gunther from the German text of Adrian Woldt. Chicago: University of Chicago Press.

Jenkins, Michael R. 1972. Glass Trade Beads in Alaska. *Alaska Journal*, vol. 2, no. 3 (Summer):31-39.

Lantis, Margaret. 1947. *Alaskan Eskimo Ceremonialism*. Seattle: University of Washington Press.

Larsen, Dinah W. 1972. Notes on the Material Culture of the Eskimos in Northwestern Alaska. In *Modern Alaskan Native Material Culture*, edited by Wendell Oswalt, 35-42. University of Alaska Museum, project report.

Larsen, Helge and Froelich Rainey. 1948. *Ipiutak and the Arctic Whale Hunting Culture*. New York: American Museum of Natural History, anthropological papers.

McCartney, Allen P. 1979. *Archaeological Whale Bone: A Northern Resource*. University of Arkansas, anthropoligical papers, no. 1:1-19.

Meldgaard, Jorgen. 1960. *Eskimo Sculpture*. New York: Clarkson N. Potter, Inc.

Milan, Frederick A. 1964. The Acculturation of the Contemporary Eskimo of Wainwright, Alaska. *Anthropoligical Papers of the University of Alaska*, vol. 2, no. 2:1-96.

Morgan, Lael, ed. *Alaska's Native People*. Anchorage: Alaska Geographic, vol. 6, no. 3.

Nelson, Edward W. 1899. *The Eskimo About Bering Strait*. Washington, D.C.: Bureau of American Ethnology Annual Report, vol. 18, part 1.

Nordenskiold, A.E. 1882. *The Voyage of the Vega Round Asia and Europe*, translated by Alexander Leslie. London: Macmillan and Co.

Oswalt, Wendell H. 1952. The Archeology of Hooper Bay Village, Alaska. *Anthropoligical Papers of the University of Alaska*, vol. 1, no. 1; 47-91.

1963. *Mission of Change in Alaska*. San Marino: The Huntington Library.

1967. *Alaskan Eskimos*. San Francisco: Chandler Publishing Co.

1972. The Eskimo (Yuk) of Western Alaska. In *Modern Alaskan Native Material Culture*, edited by Wendell Oswalt, 73-95. University of Alaska Museum, project report.

1979. *Eskimos and Explorers*. Navato, California: Chandler & Sharp Publishers, Inc.

Ray, Dorothy Jean. 1959. The Eskimo Raincoat. In *Alaska Sportsman* 25, no. 11 (November):13, 44.

1961. *Artists of the Tundra and the Sea*. Seattle: University of Washington Press.

1977. *Eskimo Art: Tradition and Innovation in North Alaska*. Seattle: University of Washington Press.

1981. *Aleut and Eskimo Art: Tradition and Innovation in South Alaska*. Seattle: University of Washington Press.

1982. Mortuary Art of the Alaskan Eskimos. In *American Indian Art 7*, no. 2 (Spring):50-57.

and Alfred R. Blaker. 1967. *Eskimo Masks: Art and Ceremony*. Seattle: University of Washington Press.

Shinkwin, Anne. 1977. *Excavations at Point Hope, Alaska—1975*. A Report to the National Park Service and the North Slope Borough (Fairbanks).

Spearman, Grant. 1979. *Anaktuvuk Pass: Land Uses Values Through Time*. Cooperative Park Studies Unit, University of Alaska, occasional paper, (Fairbanks) no. 22.

Stefansson-Anderson Arctic Expedition. (1919) 1978. Reprint, American Museum of Natural History, anthropological papers, vol. 14. New York: AMS Press.

U.S. Dept. of the Interior, final report, Bureau of Indian Affairs. 1964. *Alaska Native Arts and Crafts Potential for Expansion,* comp. George Rogers and others. Univeristy of Alaska.

Van Stone, James W. 1953. Carved Human Figures from St. Lawrence Island, Alaska. *Anthropological Papers of the University of Alaska*, vol. 2, no. 1:19-29.

Voss, Doris M. 1970. Eskimo Dolls. *Alaska Magazine*, (September):20.

Wingert, Paul S. 1962. *Primitive Art*. New York: Oxford University Press.

Selected General References

Aldrich, Herbert L. 1889. *Arctic Alaska and Siberia or Eight Months with the Arctic Whalemen*. Chicago: Rand, McNally & Co.

An Introduction to the Native Arts of Alaska. 1972. For the Anchorage Historical and Fine Arts Museum. Dept. of Parks and Recreation (Anchorage).

Anderson, J.P. 1939. Plants Used by the Eskimo of the Northern Bering Sea and Arctic Regions of Alaska. *American Journal of Botany*, 26, no. 9:714-716.

Binford, Lewis R. 1978. *Nunamiut Ethnoarchaeology*. New York: Academic Press.

Bland, Laurel J. 1972. *The Northern Eskimos of Alaska*. Alaska Methodist University.

Blomberg, Nancy, 1972. Dolls, Miniatures, and Toys. In *An Introduction to the Native Art of Alaska*, 80-81. Anchorage Historical and Fine Arts Museum.

Boaz, Franz. 1951. *Primitive Art*. New York: Capitol Publishing Co., Inc.

Brower, Charles D. 1960. *Fifty Years Below Zero*. New York: Dodd, Mead, and Co.

Carpenter, Edmund. 1973. Some Notes on the Separate Realities of Eskimo and Indian Art. In *The Far North: 2000 Years of American Eskimo and Indian Art*, 281-289. For the Anchorage Historical and Fine Arts Museum, The National Gallery of Art (Washington).

Chandonnet, Ann Fox. 1982. Six Alaskan Dollmakers. Unpublished manuscript, excerpts of which appeared in the *Anchorage Daily News, We Alaskans* (April 10).

Collins, Henry B., Jr. 1937. *Archeology of St. Lawrence Island, Alaska*. Washington: Smithsonian Institution.

Dockstader, Frederick J. The Role of the Individual Indian Artist. In *Primitive Art & Society*, edited by Anthony Forge, 113-125. London: Oxford University Press.

Dumond, Don E. 1977. *The Eskimos and Aleuts*. London: Thames and Hudson.

Erkin, Annette E. 1972. *Contact and Change*. University of Alaska Museum and NEH.

Freest, Christian F. 1980. *Native Arts of North America*. New York: Oxford University Press.

Firm, Jo Ann. 1972. Parkas. In *Alaska Magazine* 38, no. 11 (November):42-50.

Fox, Carl. 1972. *The Doll*. New York: Harry N. Abrams, Inc.

Frederick, Saradell Ard. 1972. Alaskan Eskimo Art Today. In *Alaska Journal*, vol. 2, no. 4, (Autumn):30-41 and cover.

Gerbrands, Adrian. 1969. The Concept of Style in Non-Western Art. In *Tradition and Creativity in Tribal Art*, edited by Daniel P. Biebuyck, 58-70. Berkeley: University of California Press.

Harkey, Julius M. 1959. The Shishmaref Horn Doll. In *The Alaska Sportsman* 25, no. 8:24-25.

Hippler, Arthur E., and John R. Wood. 1977. *The Alaska Eskimos: A Selected, Annotated Bibliography*. Institute of Social and Economic Research, University of Alaska (Fairbanks).

Hooper, Lt. William H., R.N. 1853. *Ten Months Among the Tents of the Tuski*. London: John Murray.

Larsen, Dinah. 1974. *Eskimo Dolls in the Collection of the University of Alaska Museum*. Poster/pamphlet (Fairbanks).

Leach, Edmund. 1973. Levels of Communications and Problems of Taboo in the Appreciation of Primitive Art. In *Primitive Art & Society*, edited by Anthony Jorge, 221-234. London: Oxford University Press.

Lipton, Barbara. 1977. *Survival: Life and Art of the Alaskan Eskimo*. Newark: The Newark Museum.

Mason, Otis Tufton. (1902) 1970. *Aboriginal Indian Basketry*. Reprint, Glorieta, New Mexico: Rio Grande Press, Inc.

More Native Art. 1971. In *Alaska Journal* 1, no. 4:31-34.

Morgan, Lael. 1973. Trade Beads. In *Alaska Journal*, 3, no. 4, (Autumn):217-225.

1974. *And The Land Provides*. New York: Anchor Press/Doubleday.

Nelson, Richard K. 1969. *Hunters of the Northern Ice*. Chicago: University of Chicago.

Oswalt, Wendell H. 1957. A Western Eskimo Ethnobotany. *Anthropoligical Papers of the University of Alaska*, vol. 6, no. 1:16-36.

1965. The Kuskokwin River Drainage, Alaska: An Annotated Bibliography. *Anthropological Papers of the University of Alaska*, vol. 13, no. 1.

Phebus, George, Jr. 1972. *Alaskan Eskimo Life in the 1890's as Sketched By Native Artists*. Washington: Smithsonian Institution Press.

Rainey, Froelich G. 1941. Eskimo Prehistory: The Okvik Site on the Punuk Islands. *Anthropological Papers of the American Museum of Natural History*, vol. 37, part 4 (New York).

Rasmussen, Knud. 1969. *Across Arctic America: Narrative of the Fifth Thule Expedition.* New York: Greenwood Press.

Ray, Dorothy Jean. 1975. *The Eskimos of Bering Strait, 1650-1898.* Seattle: University of Washington Press.

Rearden, Jim. 1979. *Yukon-Kuskokwim Delta.* Alaska Geographic, vol. 6, no. 1.

1981. *Alaska Mammals.* Alaska Geographic, vol. 8, no. 2.

Scheffer, Victor B. 1958. *Seals, Sea Lions, and Walruses.* Stanford University Press.

Schwalbe, Anna Buxbaum. 1951. *Dayspring on the Kuskokwim.* Bethelehem, PA: Moravian Press.

Silook, Roger S. 1976. *Seevookuk: Stories the Old People Told on St. Lawrence Island* (Anchorage).

Swinton, George. 1958. Eskimo Carving Today. In *The Beaver,* (Spring) Outfit 268:40-47.

U.S. Dept. of the Interior, Planning Support Group, Bureau of Indian Affairs. 1977. *Gambell: Its History, Population and Economy.* Report no. 243 (Billings, Montana).

1977. *Savoonga: Its History, Population and Economy* (Billings).

U.S. Dept. of the Interior, Office of Indian Affairs. *Catalogue of Alaskan Native Craft Products* (Juneau).

Van Valin, William B. 1944. *Eskimoland Speaks.* Caldwell, Idaho: The Caxton Printers, Ltd.

Weyer, Edward Moffat Jr. 1962. *The Eskimos: Their Environment and Folkways.* Hamden: Archon Books.

Wilder, Edna. 1976. *Secrets of Eskimo Skinsewing.* Anchorage: Alaska Northwest Publishing Co.

Yupiktak Bista. 1974. *Does One Way of Life Have to Die So Another Can Live?* Report of subsistence and the conservation of the Yupik lifestyle.

Alaska State Council on the Arts